Wisdom of Chanakya

(1001 Sparks)

BOOKS BY V.K. SUBRAMANIAN

Religion & Philosophy
Sri Rudraprasna
Saundaryalahari of Sankaracharya
Sivanandalahari of Sankaracharya
The Upanishads and the Bible
Raja Yoga – The Royal Road to Revelation

Indian Culture
Art Shrines of Ancient India
Sacred Songs of India (Volumes 1 to 10)
Wondrous Whispers of Wisdom from Ancient India (Volumes 1 to 3)
Maxims of Chanakya
Mystic Songs of Meera
Hymns of Tulsidas

Astrology/Palmistry
Predictive Planets and Presaging Palms

Health Management
The Holistic Way to Health, Happiness and Harmony
Heavenly Living Here & Now

Biography
The Great Ones (Volumes 1 to 10)
The Great Ones of India
101 Mystics of India

Economy/Finance
The Indian Financial System
Introspection for India – A Paradigm for Progress

Fiction
A Feeling for Feminism
Lali and Other Short Stories
Love Twigs
A Bond to Sorrow

Wisdom of Chanakya

(1001 Sparks)

V.K. SUBRAMANIAN

ABHINAV
PUBLICATIONS

abhinav publications
NEW DELHI

Cataloging in Publication Data—DK
Courtesy: D.K. Agencies (P) Ltd. <docinfo@dkagencies.com>

Kautòalya.
[Selections. English & Sanskrit]
Wisdom of Chanakya : 1001 sparks / [compiled by] V.K. Subramanian.
p. cm.
English and Sanskrit.
Includes bibliographical references (p.).
ISBN 8170175321

1. Political science—India—History. 2. India—Politics and government—To 997. 3. India—Social conditions—To 1200. I. Subramanian, V. K., 1930- II. Title.

DDC 320.1 23

First published in India 2012

Publishers
Shakti Malik
Abhinav Publications
E-37, Hauz Khas
New Delhi-110016 (INDIA)
Phones: 26566387, 26524658
Fax: 91-11-26857009
e-mail: abhinavpublications@airtelmail.in
website: http//www.abhinavpublications.net

ISBN 81-7071-532-1

Lasertypeset by
R.S. Prints
Gautam Nagar, New Delhi-110049

Printed at
Star Print-o-Bind
Okhla, Phase-I, New Delhi

To

Late C.V. Swaminathan

who was so lovable in his humility and

helpfulness to everyone

Contents

CHANAKYA

Introductory Remarks of Chanakya to His Work: Chanakya Niti

प्रणम्य शिरसा विष्णुं त्रैलोक्याधिपतिं प्रभुम्।
नानाशास्त्रोद्धतं वक्ष्ये राजनीतिसमुच्चयम्॥

Prostrating before Lord Vishnu, who is the Ruler of the three worlds, I am presenting this compendium of political science, collected from various scriptures.

अधीत्येवं यथाशास्त्रं नरों जानाति सत्तय।
धर्मोपदेशविख्यातं कार्याऽकार्य शूभाश्भम्॥

Studying this, a man learns what to do or not to do! What is good and what is not, in essence, the whole gamut of advice on righteousness.

तदहं संप्रवक्ष्यामि लोकानां हित्तकाम्यया।
येन विज्ञानमात्रेण सर्वज्ञत्वं प्रपद्यते॥

I am presenting what is good for the world, by which people can become totally knowledgeable.

Introduction

(Chanakya: His Life, Times and Work)

Chanakya, also known as Kautilya and Vishnugupta, was the famous Indian Machiavelli who was responsible for the overthrow of the last ruler of the Nanda Dynasty and the enthronement of Chandragupta Maurya. Brahmin by caste, he roughly lived during the period 350-275 B.C.

There is an interesting story about Chanakya's first encounter with Chandragupta, which ultimately ended in their collaboration and capture of power.

One day when Chandragupta who had been dismissed from Nanda's army was walking through the forest he saw a Brahmin pouring sugar syrup on the roots of Kusa grass. Rendered curious, Chandragupta asked Chanakya the rationale of his action, Chanakya replied: "This Kusa grass hurt my leg, I hence intend to destroy it. By pouring sugar syrup, I am rendering the root of the grass sweet. As a result, thousands of ants will be attracted to it. These ants will nibble at and destroy the root and the grass will die."

Even as he spoke, the ants started collecting and soon there was an army of ants around the root of the Kusa grass which had hurt Chanakya. Chandragupta bowed his head before the sagacity and foresight of Chanakya and pleaded for his help and advice in becoming a Ruler. Chanakya, who already bore a grudge against Nanda, readily agreed.

Chanakya helped Chandragupta in raising a large army and defeating Nanda. After making him the Emperor of India, Chanakya functioned as his

Counsellor and advised him in all matters of the State.

With the able advice of Chanakya, Chandragupta Maurya ruled for twenty-four years.

Biographical details available about Chanakya are scanty. We have mainly to rely on tradition, and the Buddhist and Jain texts of later periods.

Chanakya's place of birth is a matter of controversy. The Mahavamsa Tika, a Ceylonese Buddhist work, mentions Taxila as his birthplace, while Hemachandra the Jain writer in his "Abhidhanachintamani" says that Chanakya, son of Chanaka, was a Dramila, that is, an inhabitant of South India.

There is another version that the name Chanakya is derived from the name of his native land (some place called Chanaka in the Punjab) as per a statement in the Jayamangala commentary on the Nitisara.

A place called "Gollavishaya" has also been mentioned as the birthplace of Chanakya in the "Parisishtaparvan".

Kerala has also staked a claim as the homeland of Chanakya on the basis that his tuft was that of a Nambudhiri Brahmin.

Since Alexander's campaigns were predominantly in the Punjab and Plutarch has gone on record that Alexander had met Chandragupta as a youth during his campaigns, it would be safer to accept the version that Takshasila (Taxila) in the Punjab was the native city of Chanakya, where he and Chandragupta spent several years together.

Though the story about the encounter between Chanakya and Chandragupta mentioned at the beginning of this introduction is the popular one, according to Buddhist texts and traditions, accepted by historians, the version is that Chanakya found Chandragupta in a village as the adopted son of a cowherd from whom he bought the boy by paying on the spot 1,000 *Karsapanas*, seeing in him the sure promise of future greatness. Chanakya is supposed to have taken the young Chandragupta with him to his native city of Takshasila (Taxila), then the most renowned seat of learning in India and had him educated there for a period of seven or eight years in the Humanities and the Practical Arts and Crafts of the time, including the Military Arts.

Despite the apparent contradictions in the various legends and traditions about Chanakya and Chandragupta as Prof. K.A. Nilakanta Sastri points out: "There is little reason to doubt the truth of the main story in its outline: An unusually valiant Kshatriya Warrior and a Brahmin Statesman of great learning and resourcefulness joined to bring about the downfall of an avaricious dynasty of hated rulers, and establish a new empire which made the good of the people its chief concern; they freed the land from the foreign invader, and from internal tyranny, and established a State which, in due course, embraced practically the whole of India; together they organized one of the most powerful and efficient bureaucracies known to the history of the world. Kshatra (imperium) and Brahma (sacerdotium) came together and engaged in the most fruitful cooperation for the great good of the land and the people."

Indian epigraphical researches confirm 321 B.C. as the year in which Chandragupta Maurya was enthroned as King. It would hence be safe to assume that Chanakya's works were produced during the period 321 B.C. to 290 B.C.

The "Arthasastra", a treatise on the science of politics, is the most famous work of Chanakya. Though it is more often known as Kautilya's Arthasastra, the authorship of Chanakya is unmistakable.

There is a reference to Chanakya's Arthasastra in the Panchatantra. In an introduction to his work, the author of Panchatantra refers to the Dharmasastras of Manu, the Arthasastras of Chanakya and the Kamasutras of Vatsyayana and others.

That Kautilya and Chanakya are one and the same person has been universally accepted by all historians.

The Maxims of Chanakya translated in this book are based on three works: "Chanakyasutras", "Chanakyanitidarpana", and "Arthasastra".

The similarity of language and the identity of expression discernible in the first two works and the Arthasastra leaves no doubt about the common authorship.

In Dandi's famous work "Dasakumaracharita" there is a reference to the Arthasastra of Vishnugupta. The relevant passage runs thus: "Learn now the science of politics. This has been summarized into six thousand verses for the benefit of Maurya Kings by the venerable teacher Vishnugupta. Learning this well and practising it properly, one requires the competence to deal with various tasks."

The fact that the Arthasastra contains 6,000 verses confirms the identity of Vishnugupta and Chanakya.

That Chanakya was the Chief Minister of Chandragupta Maurya is mentioned in Megasthenes' account of India: "Indika". Since it is generally accepted by historians that the Greek historian came to India towards the end of the fourth century B.C., as the Ambassador of Seleucus Nicator, the Greek General of Alexander, who was defeated by Chandragupta Maurya in battle and with whom a treaty was signed ceding the territories of Kabul, Kandahar and Baluchistan to the victor, it would appear unnecessary to doubt the period in which Chanakya lived and produced his brilliant works dealing with statecraft and the various facets of public administration and private life.

Efforts have, however, been made by scholars to prove that Chanakya's works belong not to the fourth century B.C. but to the third century A.D. It is hence considered necessary to examine the grounds on which doubts about the date of the works have been raised.

Since the period during which Chandragupta

Maurya and Chanakya lived has been proved on the basis of historical evidence and epigraphical researches, the major ground open to skeptics is to question the authorship of Chanakya and to claim that these Maxims and Aphorisms are the work of later authors erroneously attributed to Chanakya.

The intellectual genius of Chanakya was so towering and elicited so much adulation in his own time and subsequently that attempts were not infrequently made to identify him as the author of several works dealing with a variety of subjects ranging from sex to astronomy and mathematics.

Thus Hemachandra in his "Abhidhanachintamani" propounded the theory that Chanakya was the same Vatsyayana, the author of Kamasutra, apart from being an Astronomer, Mathematician and Logician.

The scope for such assumptions has arisen from some passages in Kamasutra which are similar to those in Arthasastra.

For example, both Kamasutra and Arthasastra refer to the three divisions of Artha or Wealth: "Artho Dharmah Kama Ithyarthatrivargah" ("Riches, righteousness and love are the three aspects of wealth").

That no aspect of learning was left untouched by Chanakya is clear from the maxims attributed to him. Thus, while his forte was politics and administration, he knew enough about ethics, morality, psychology, sex, dietetics etc. but to attribute the authorship of subsequent works like Kamasutra to Chanakya and thus create confusion about the date of his own works would be incorrect.

All knowledge and wisdom is a legacy handed over from one generation to another – through word of mouth rather than the written word in the olden days – that not infrequently subsequent authors borrowed ideas and idioms from their illustrious predecessors.

Thus merely because there are some isolated passages in Kamasutra reminiscent of verses in

Arthasastra, it would be indefensible to argue that since the date of Kamasutra is being taken as the fourth century A.D., Chanakya's works could not belong to a much earlier period.

Similar is the case with reference to the mention of Chanakya's works in Kamandaka's "*Nitisara*", a work believed to have been transported into the island of Bali by Indian immigrants in fourth century A.D. Efforts have also been made, on the basis of certain passages in Kalidasa's works, to prove that Kalidasa and Chanakya belonged to the same period. Some have even gone to the extent of claiming that the two were one and the same person.

It is true that the indebtedness of Kalidasa to Chanakya is proved beyond doubt by the fact that Kalidasa's "Raghuvamsa" contains many words which are used in a technical sense in the Arthasastra. Examples are: *Sastra, Danda, Dandaniti, Prakriti, Mantra, Saptanga, Kosa Mandala* etc.

Dr. Raghavan, the eminent Sanskrit scholar of the Madras University in his paper on "Kalidasa and Kautilya" (read before the thirteenth session of the All India Oriental Conference held at the Nagpur University in 1946), has cited a number of instances of parallel ideas in the works of the two and remarks: "All these presuppose that Kalidasa had before him some texts on Polity in which there was a large mass of technical terms whose meanings were well defined and which had, therefore, come to be well understood."

By a detailed analysis, Dr. Raghavan has proved that the most important of the texts on Polity which Kalidasa had with him was the Arthasastra of Chanakya.

This only indicates that Chanakya lived many years before Kalidasa and there is no evidence to dispute Chanakya's contemporaneity with Chandragupta Maurya, whose enthronement in 321 B.C. is generally accepted by historians.

Chanakya functioned as the Chief Minister of Chandragupta Maurya between 323 and 298 B.C. and it would not be unreasonable to assume that Chanakya composed his great works after retiring from active politics, that is, after he successfully consolidated the Maurya empire and made his rival Rakshasa the Chief Minister of Chandragupta Maurya. On this basis, Chanakya's works belong to the third century B.C.

Since conclusive evidence exists to show that Chanakya's works could not be later than third century A.D., disputes about the date of Chanakya's works get narrowed down to a period of six centuries. We may leave researchers and scholars to sift evidence and come to some firm conclusion, if and when they desire.

As far as we, on the threshold of twenty-first century, are concerned, we may derive satisfaction that we have been bequeathed works of wisdom, which are nearly two thousand years old, and we may attempt to learn how much of these are relevant to modern times and can be used with advantage by those who shape a country's destiny or an individual's future.

In this light, all arguments concerning the date of Chanakya's works or whether he was born in South India assume less importance than a critical study of the texts which are available to us and which after editing by various scholars are broadly attributed to him. Before we attempt to study these works, we may try to make an assessment of Chanakya, the man, who played a dominating part in the establishment, growth and preservation of the Maurya empire.

Opinions differ on the type of person that Chanakya was. The common concept is that of a crafty politician, the "Brahmin Fox" who cared little for means in the achievement of ends. The strongest condemnation of the man who destroyed the powerful Nanda kings and put Chandragupta Maurya on the throne and consolidated his empire by the fusion of several petty States comes from Bana, the author of *Kadambari*, who says: "Is there anything that is righteous for those for whom the science of Kautilya, merciless in its precepts, rich in cruelty, is an authority, whose teachers are priests, habitually hard hearted with practice of witchcraft, to whom ministers, always inclined to deceive others, are councillors, whose desire is always for the Goddess of wealth that has been cast away by thousands of kings, who are devoted to the application of destructive sciences, and to whom brothers, affectionate with natural cordial love, are fit victims to be murdered?"

One would realize that Bana's judgment of Chanakya was harsh when one recalls the historical perspective and the role of Chanakya with reference to the political conditions which prevailed in the country at the time.

As Dr. R.K. Mukherji narrates in his article, "The Foundation of the Mauryan Empire", "The country had hardly recovered from the shock of Alexander's victorious march through it – a march which had dislocated its indigenous political organization. It had already passed under the grip and stranglehold of foreign rule. The atmosphere was full of frustration and depression. The battle of India's Independence against these heavy odds called for a leader of exceptional ability and vision who would infuse new life and enthusiasm into the drooping spirits of a defeated people, and organize a fresh national resistance against alien domination. Fortunately the country produced such a leader in young Chandragupta who had already been prepared in advance for his great mission in life by the Brahmin Chanakya, better known as Kautilya. Chanakya's superior vision and insight led him to discover in this youth the disciple who would be able, under his direction, to free the fatherland of foreign rule."

A correct assessment of Chanakya's personality is given by Jawaharlal Nehru in his "Discovery of India".

He writes: "Chanakya has been called the Indian Machiavelli and to some extent the comparison is justified. But he was a much bigger person in every way, greater in intellect and action. He was no mere follower of a King, a humble adviser of an all powerful emperor." A picture of him emerges from an old Indian play, "The Mudra Rakshasa" which deals with this period. Bold and scheming, proud and revengeful, never forgetting a slight, never forgetting his purpose, availing himself of every device to delude and defeat the enemy, he sat with the reins of empire in his hands and looked upon the emperor more as a loved pupil than as a master.

"Simple and austere in his life, uninterested in the pomp and pageantry of high position, when he had redeemed his pledge and accomplished his purpose, he wanted to retire, Brahmin like, to a life of contemplation."

There was hardly anything Chanakya would have refrained from doing to achieve his purpose; he was unscrupulous enough, yet he was also wise enough to know that this very purpose might be defeated by means unsuited to the end. Long before Clausewitz, he is reported to have said that war is only a continuance of State policy by other means. But he adds, war must always serve the larger ends of policy and not become an end in itself. The statesman's objective must always be the betterment of the State as a result of war and not the mere defeat and destruction of the enemy.

If war involves both parties in a common ruin, that is the bankruptcy of statesmanship. War must be conducted by armed forces but much more important than the force of arms is the high strategy which saps the enemy's morale and disrupts his forces and brings about his collapse or takes him to the verge of collapse before armed attack.

Unscrupulous and rigid as Chanakya was in the

pursuit of his aim, he never forgot that it was better to win over an intelligent and high-minded enemy than to crush him. His final victory was obtained by sowing discord in the enemy's ranks and in the very moment of his victory, so the story goes, he induced Chandragupta to be generous to his rival chief. Chanakya himself is said to have handed over the insignia of his own high office to the Minister of that rival whose intelligence and loyalty to his old chief had impressed him greatly. So the story ends not in the bitterness of defeat and humiliation, but in reconciliation and in laying the firm and enduring foundations of a State, which had not only defeated but won over its chief enemy.

Chanakya's amazing knowledge of human psychology, his masterly insight into every facet of human life – and not merely his political wisdom and statesmanship – can be seen reflected in the Maxims, translated in this volume.

There is an ethical undertone in his thought and teaching. In the Arthasastra, which, like Machiavelli's Prince, has often been misunderstood, he says: "Kritsnam Hi Sastramidamindriyajayah" ("The crux of this political science is control over senses").

The ideal ruler, according to Chanakya, should have absolute mastery over himself and be "pre-eminent in virtue" – not very different from the ideal monarch, Aristotle, a contemporary of Chanakya, envisaged or the philosopher king which Plato visualized. The effect of the quality and character of the ruler on the people he rules over has been repeatedly emphasized by Chanakya:

"If rulers are righteous, people are righteous, if they are sinners, people are also sinners, like ruler, like people."

"A ruler with character can render even unendowed people happy. A characterless ruler destroys loyal and prosperous people."

"It is better not to have a ruler than a bad ruler. Where is happiness for the people in a State ruled by a bad ruler?"

It is not enough for the ruler to have merely good character. He must be well-versed in the various sciences of State. He must be adept in political science. Only by practising political science can he protect the people. A ruler not proficient in the various sciences is not fit to hear ministerial counsel, He will act indiscriminately, be obstinate in decisions and will be led by others.

Chanakya has likened the ruler devoid of learning, advised by an unwise minister to "A mad elephant, mounted by an intoxicated mahout, which tramples on everything it comes across."

Even a well-endowed, intelligent and learned ruler needs counsel and advice. Says Chanakya: "Governance is possible only with assistance. A single wheel does not move. Hence ministers should be appointed and their counsel listened to."

This is reminiscent of Zoroaster's dictum: "A knife of the keenest steel requires the whetstone and the wisest man needs advice."

What type of persons should be appointed as counsellors? "A ruler should appoint as counsellor one who respects him, one who is learned and who is free from fraud", advises Chanakya.

He is against the appointment of classmates as ministers; for, though trustworthy, they will not respect the ruler, having been playmates.

According to Chanakya a country prospers out of abundant ministerial advice, "which should be kept secret from all quarters."

The ruler is advised to take a decision on the unanimous opinion of three counsellors.

How does a ruler win over the people? "Exercise of

power and achievement of result should be properly matched by the ruler in order to win over the people. He should adopt the same mode of life, same dress, same language and same customs as those of the people."

Factors which create discontent among the people have been listed by Chanakya as under:

"Disrespect shown to good people and encouragement of the unrighteous; acts of unprecedented and unrighteous violence, stoppage of righteous and appropriate customs, encouragement of vice and discouragement of virtue, not punishing the guilty and severely punishing the innocent, doing what ought not to be done and preventing what ought to be done, arresting those who should not be arrested and not arresting those deserving to be arrested, undertaking schemes which result in loss and stopping those which would result in gain, accepting donations which should not be taken and not giving donations which ought to be given, harming important leaders of the people and dishonouring respectable ones, estrangement of elders, nepotism, falsehood etc. etc.

Even today we find Governments indulging in the tabooed activities listed by Chanakya becoming unpopular and falling from power due to the discontent of the people.

Unlike Louis XIV who identified himself with the State and came to ruin, Chanakya stresses the importance of the people vis-à-vis the State. He asks: "Without people what will the State yield? Like a barren cow, nothing."

Though the ruler should be righteous, Chanakya does not want him to be either weak or impoverished.

A weak ruler, even if learned, is not respected by the people. Apt punishment, the root of discipline, should be meted out by the ruler, so that the people do not commit crime and function properly in their respective spheres. "He who punishes mildly is despised", was the view held by Chanakya, which tallies with Napoleon's theory that "When men call a king a kind man, his reign has been a failure."

Both in internal administration and foreign policy, Chanakya recommended the deployment of the fourfold policy of "conciliation, donation, division and punishment".

In Chanakya's times, neighbouring States were most relevant in foreign policy. Chanakya makes the significant observation:

"A ruler with contiguous territory is a rival. The ruler next to the adjoining one is to be deemed a friend", which has proved to be mostly true even in modern times, which has witnessed major conflagrations flare up from clashes between bordering States.

In the matter of war, Chanakya's advice is: "One should fight with an inferior but sign a treaty of peace with one's equal and superior." What are the weak States to do in the circumstances? "The weak should seek refuge in the strong."

Chanakya gives elaborate advice as to how enemies should be tackled. "When there are many enemies, treaty should be entered into with one." "One should offer to one enemy that which is likely to be taken by force by another enemy."

It is interesting to compare Chanakya's approach in this regard with Clausewitz's. Both are agreed that attention should be concentrated on one enemy, among the many. But while Chanakya advises stratagem and treaty with one, Clausewitz advocates outright war: "We may establish it as a principle that if we conquer all our enemies by conquering one of them, the defeat of that one must be the aim of the war, because it is that one we hit the common centre of gravity of the whole war."

Chanakya sought to achieve without bloodshed what Clausewitz aimed at through war.

Chanakya attached great importance to efficient administration and speedy accomplishment of tasks. "The ruler should attend to all urgent matters promptly and never postpone them. A matter deferred consideration and decision becomes more difficult or impossible to tackle." "Every morning the day's tasks should be planned. Tomorrow's deed should be done today. What is to be done in the afternoon should be done in the forenoon."

As a rational intellectual, whose emphasis was always on result-oriented action, Chanakya scorned blind belief in stars and destiny. He said: "One who desires speedy accomplishment of tasks does not look to the stars to know his fortune. Rational prognostics are superior to stars in guidance."

Despite his involvement in political manoeuvring and State stratagems, Chanakya never lost sight of the larger perspectives of life.

To him, as to his fellow countrymen even to this day, life had its fourfold objective *Dharma* (righteous duty), *Artha* (acquisition of wealth), *Kama* (enjoyment of pleasures) and *Moksha* (liberation from worldly bondage).

On each of these objectives of life, Chanakya dwells at length and renders sound advice. According to him, equal attention should be paid to the performance of righteous duty, acquisition of material wealth and enjoyment of physical pleasures. "Any one of the three, if excessively indulged in, harms itself and the other two." Also, material wealth is the most important, since performance of righteous duty and enjoyment of pleasures are dependent on it. Hence all types of riches should be amassed by all means, so as to enable the attainment of other objectives in life.

A society or country is composed of various

elements: the ruler and the ruled, the men and women, the husbands and wives, the parents and children, the teachers and the taught, the intellectuals, the soldiers, the business class and the people engaged in services.

The harmony and happiness of the whole country and the community depend on the proper discharge of duties by the people functioning in their respective spheres. Any discordant element anywhere disrupts the whole structure.

Thus the duty of the ruler is to keep the people happy and prosperous, while the people in their turn should obey the orders of the ruler and not go against him.

Similarly, the preceptors, the soldiers, the business class and the people engaged in services should perform their assigned duties.

Parents should provide maximum education to their children. "That mother and that father are enemies who do not give education to their children", says Chanakya.

The children should obey their parents and look after them, when they are in difficulties.

Teachers should teach only those things which conduce to righteousness and material prosperity. "Teaching wrong things is a great crime." The student should respect the teacher, serve him well and be ever grateful to him for the knowledge imparted.

Husbands should sexually satisfy their wives and wives in their turn should be "pure and chaste" and serve their husbands well.

Chanakya stresses the need for ceaseless activity for the acquisition of wealth, "the root of righteousness". "By undertaking all kinds of activities, the ways to profit develop." "One should earn wealth as if one is immortal." He despises the inactive who look to the stars for fortune. "Wealth will desert the childish man who always consults the stars."

Righteous means are, however, not to be disregarded in acquiring wealth. "Wealth earned through unlawful means lasts for ten years. In the eleventh year it is completely lost", says Chanakya. "Wealth earned should not be stored, but spent." "Spending riches earned is saving, like the removal of water stored in the body of tank." In this advice, Chanakya is in the good company of George Washington who said: "It is not a custom with me to keep money to look at."

Chanakya went further and pointed out: "Enjoyment adorns wealth." He also advocated liberal donation of enjoyable wealth to good recipients.

In the enjoyment of material pleasures, Chanakya advocated moderation and adherence to the path of righteousness. While a happy one with a good wife, obedient sons, good friends were all considered as essential elements of happiness, excessive addiction to women, gambling, hunting etc. was frowned upon.

Control over senses is a theme constantly stressed as a prerequisite for all achievement. The sage-statesman, who helped establish the first Indian empire and was ruthless in dealing with enemies, was himself an austere bachelor and retired to a life of seclusion and contemplation, as soon as his political objectives were achieved.

The philosophic emphasis on the transience of life and the need for liberation from worldly bondage and the cycle of birth and death, the constant exhortation to give up sensory pleasures and develop qualities of patience, kindness, purity and truth may sound unreal, coming as they do from the lips of the man who advocated the amassing of wealth, "as if one is immortal", but can be understood if one bears in mind the Indian concept of the four stages of life, through which one is expected to proceed from birth to liberation.

The first stage is *Brahmacharya*, the stage of celibacy during which one is expected to acquire learning, with single-minded devotion to the teacher and leading a life of discipline and purity.

The second stage is *Grahastya*, the age of the householder, when one enjoys physical pleasures and domestic bliss, in the prime of one's life, when the senses demand satisfaction.

The third stage is called *Vanaprastha*, the life of retirement in the forest, where the husband and wife live in each other's company, leading a life of prayer and meditation, having tasted the sweetest pleasures, begotten children and grandchildren, the body's hungers having been satisfied fully, the need now being to seek mental solace and spirituality.

The fourth stage is *Sannyasa*, the stage of renunciation when everything is given up and one feels completely detached from the world, ready to merge with the Supreme, of which the individual is a part.

It is in the light of the above that the fourfold objective of life becomes meaningful: One performs righteous duty, whether that duty is ruling a State or an organization, teaching in a university, serving in the armed forces, running a business or serving the community. In the due discharge of such duty one earns wealth and enjoys all the pleasures which the body desires and needs and finally in the ripeness of age, tries to seek moksha or liberation from earthly bondage by leading a life of prayer, meditation and spirituality.

It is not necessary, according to Indian thinking with which Chanakya entirely seems to agree, to keep the different objectives of life in watertight compartments. One could lead an integrated life, properly balancing the sensual and the spiritual needs.

This brief introduction would be incomplete if a tribute is not paid to the sweep and range of Chanakya's wisdom and his keen observation of natural phenomena, from which ethical and moral conclusions are drawn and lessons in human psychology imparted. A few of his maxims would illustrate this point:

"Just as a calf goes to its mother, seeking her out from among thousands of cows, so every action follows the doer."

"Even the fangless serpent should raise its hood, for with or without position, a raised hood is frightening."

"From the cock one should learn four things: getting up in time, fighting, division of responsibility among relations and enjoyment after attacking oneself."

"From the crow one should learn five things: sex in secrecy, secret action, catch in time, unruffled behaviour and distrust of everyone."

"Just as a pigeon which has lived on the holy fig tree is a source of constant danger to the silk cotton tree, so a person who has come after living with the enemy is a source of constant danger."

"Six are the qualities of the dog: desire for much, satisfaction with a little, deep slumber, quick awakening, devotion to master and bravery."

"From the donkey three things should be learnt: to carry the burden even though tired, not to mind heat or cold and to trudge ever satisfied."

"The mirage looks like water. An enemy can look like a friend."

"The cloud which rains heavily is defeated by a cluster of grass."

"The enemy can be defeated by a combination of good people."

"In the fight between the dog and the pig, the ultimate victory is that of the pariah who get the meat to eat."

"A dog on land drags the crocodile. A crocodile in water drags the dog. The place of fight is important."

"Unheated metal does not coalesce with metal. Power is the cause of an alliance."

"If the best seeking a gift were thrown away by the wild elephant with his ears, only his temples lost their adornment. The bees live again in full-blown lotuses."

"The fish, the toad and the birds protect their infants by sight, thought and touch – so do good men."

"If one goes to the lion's den, one gets ivory. If one goes to the jackal's hiding place, one gets goat's tail and donkey skin."

"Sandalwood does not give up its fragrance even if broken, the elephant does not give up sex even if old, sugarcane does not give up its sweetness even when thrown into the crushing machine. Great ones do not give up their good qualities even when they are weakened."

"One should learn from the lion to undertake a task well prepared even if it be a big task."

"The bee is capable of cutting wood, but it is harmless in the lotus-bed. There are many bonds. But the bond of love is something different." "Swans stay at a place when there is water. They abandon it when it dries up. Men should not be like swans abandoning and seeking places."

"As the fisherman catches fish from water, utilizable resources should be captured."

"As the tortoise withdraws its limbs, the ruler should try to hide any part of his which might have been exposed."

"An entire forest gets fragrant by a single flowering tree, like a family by a good son."

"The milk-seeking calf strikes at the mother's udders. Those who seek to achieve things should show no mercy."

"One should not place trust in rivers, in animals with horns, in armed ones, in women or in ruling families."

The sweep and range of Chanakya's razorsharp intellect would be self-evident by the variety of subjects dealt with in his works, from sex to scholastics, ethics to economics, politics to philosophy.

What amazes one, however, is not merely the

versatility of the man but the accuracy, relevance and applicability of his dicta, even after the lapse of two thousand years.

For example, his cryptic observation: "Lack of sex ages women" cannot be controverted even by modern psychologists and is an anticipation of the work of Freud, Havelock Ellis, Kinsey, Marie Stopes and several others who have only recently unravelled the mysteries of the human mind and body. The eternal wisdom contained in the maxim "Anger is the origin of all legal disputes, murder also results from anger", holds good for all time and in all countries.

The advice that "One should not argue with intelligent, the foolish, friends, teachers and the beloved" is Dale Carnegie's philosophy transmitted two thousand years in advance.

The dictum that "There is no attraction equal to a gift" is made capital of by commercial concerns and publicity agents the world over to sell products with gift incentives – an appreciation of the human failing, which looks forward to free gifts, even if they be of such a trivial nature as new year calendars, diaries or pencil sets or key chains.

The maxim that "No other wealth can equal food-grains" is a right reminder to nations not to neglect their agriculture, as without adequate food production, a nation's economy cannot be set on the path to prosperity.

The observation that "The treasury has its source in the mines" stresses the need for the State to exploit its natural resources, whether these comprise coal, iron, oil or non-ferrous metals.

One could go on and on with such illustrations to prove Chanakya's farsightedness, keenness of perception and infallibility. It would, however, be incorrect to assume that Chanakya's thinking was not limited, in certain aspects, by the social milieu of his time.

This is specially true of his views on women. Chanakya lived in a patriarchal, male-superior society and this naturally coloured his views on women.

A similar failing can be noticed among most of the master thinkers of the world, from Socrates to Shakespeare, from Seneca to Shaw.

If Chanakya says: "Women are fickle-minded", so has Shakespeare remarked: "Frailty thy name is woman!" Feminists may, however, derive satisfaction that Chanakya has also said: "Men's minds are not steady."

While Chanakya has listed the weaknesses of the "Weaker Vessel" (that they cannot judge men etc.) he has also paid a tribute to the "Crown of creation", by pointing out that "There is no jewel equal to a good woman."

Our disagreement with some of the views of Chanakya need not deter us from admiring the intellectual capacity of one, who could express himself so forcefully and effectively that even while disagreeing, we are forced to enjoy his remarks, full of wit and wisdom.

The message of Chanakya, stripped of all external embellishments, can be summed up in a few words: "Develop character and self-control, be ceaselessly active, be fearless and endlessly strive to attain your objectives." This is a message, ageless in quality, inspiring both for individuals and nations, a message which has come from the lips of great leaders, of all countries and all climes who have led their countrymen from darkness to light, from slavery to freedom, from poverty to prosperity.

In China, a few hundred years before Chanakya, the learned Confucius said: "There are three marks of a superior man: being virtuous, he is free from anxiety, being wise, he is free from perplexity, being brave, he is free from fear."

In Greece, almost at the same time, Pythagoras

taught: "It is only necessary to make war with five things: with the maladies of the body, the ignorances of the mind, with the passions of the body, with the seditions of the city and the discords of families."

Chanakya's wisdom contains enough ammunition to fight the wars mentioned by Pythagoras and to become the superior man of Confucius' vision.

In our own times, in India, the action-oriented philosophy of Chanakya has been restated by Swami Vivekananda, in his memorable words: "Can anything be done unless everybody exerts himself to his utmost? It is the man of action, the lion heart that the Goddess of wealth resorts to. No need of looking behind. Forward! We want infinite energy, infinite zeal, infinite courage and infinite patience. Then only will great things be achieved."

To historians, Chanakya is the intriguing, fascinating, statesman-diplomat, who, along with Chandragupta Maurya, helped establish the first unified State in Indian history and prevented the balkanization of a continent, ravaged by foreign invasions.

To students of political thought and science, Chanakya compels comparison with Machiavelli, Plato and Aristotle. In fact it would not be inappropriate to say that Chanakya was to Chandragupta what Aristotle was to Alexander.

But such assessments would be incomplete and partial. Myth and legend, tradition and history have enveloped Chanakya, the man, in mists of glory, awe, wonder and fear. It is difficult to sift fact from fiction and arrive at a true picture of the man. This need not make us despair. As Gustave Flaubert wrote to George Sand, "*L'Homme Ciest Rien, L'oeuvre C'est Tout*" ("The man is nothing, his work is everything"). While the material about Chanakya, the man, may be fragmentary, his works are very much with us, handed down from generation to generation during the last two thousand years, aided by the great Sanskrit language, in which his thoughts were expressed.

(In terseness of expression, no language, with the possible exception of Latin, can excel Sanskrit and the great master has used this wonderful language to such perfection that one is awestruck by the volume of message often conveyed in a couple of words.)

Chanakya, the thinker, belongs not only to India, "his dear and precious native land" to which he held and from which he derived the strong roots of his strength but to all the world, which needs his wisdom, even in this age of the space and the atom.

With pride and humility, I offer *Wisdom of Chanakya* (*1001 Sparks*) to my readers.

V.K. Subramanian

Chennai, 2008

Acknowledgements

My thanks are due to the University of Mysore and the Adyar Library and Research Centre, whose critically edited Sanskrit texts have been used in the writing of this book.

I am also grateful to Dr. V. Raghavan, Head of Department of Sanskrit, University of Madras, who helped me with a number of books, without which it would have been impossible for me to complete this book.

I am also indebted to Sri S. Ramakrishnan, Editor, Bhavan's Journal for kindly permitting me to use in book form some of the maxims serialized in the Bhavan's Journal between July 1972 and December 1973.

V.K. Subramanian

1
Polity and Governance

From Arthasastra

॥ श्रीः ॥

चाणक्यअर्थशास्त्र

1. Rulers: Duties and Qualities

प्रजासुखे सुखं राज्ञः प्रजानां च हिते हितम्।
नात्मप्रिय हितं राज्ञः प्रजानां तु प्रियं हितम्॥1॥

In the happiness of the people lies the ruler's happiness. Their welfare is his welfare. The ruler shall not consider what pleases and benefits him personally, but what is pleasing and beneficial to the people.

शक्तिं सिद्धिं च घटेतात्मन्यावेशयितुम्॥2॥

Exercise of power and achievement of results should be properly matched by the ruler in order to win over the people.

पड्वर्गवशगा बहवो राजानो विनष्टाः
तेषामनात्मक्तां नाहति मार्गमनुगन्तुम्
धर्ममर्थं चावेक्षस्व॥3॥

Many rulers have been destroyed by being under the control of the group of six enemies (lust, anger, greed, infatuation, arrogance, envy). Those with character should not follow their path, but preserve righteousness and wealth.

गुरुव्यसनं न्यायवृत्तिमभियुक्तं प्रकृतयोनुगृह्लन्ति॥4॥

The people help the ruler who is just in his actions, when attacked while in a serious calamity.

कृत्स्नं हि शास्त्रमिद भिन्द्रियजयः।
तद्विरुद्धवृत्तिः अवश्येन्द्रियः चातुरन्तोऽपि
राजा सद्यो विनश्यति॥5॥

The whole of this science is intended to create control over the senses. A ruler acting contrary to it and hence not having the senses under control immediately gets destroyed, even if he be the lord of the four ends of the earth.

प्रायश्च कोपवशाः राजानः प्रकृतिकोपैर्हताः श्रूयन्ते।
कामवशाः क्षयव्यसननिमित्तमरिव्याधिभिः॥6॥

Generally rulers swayed by anger have been killed by people's fury, it is heard. Those addicted to carnal pleasures have been destroyed by enemies and diseases caused by decadence and vice.

यथा मदान्धो हस्ती मत्तेनाधिष्ठितः
यद्यदासादयति तत्सर्वं प्रमृद्गाति
एवमयमशास्त्रचक्षु रन्धो राजा अन्धन
मन्त्रिणाधिष्ठतः॥7॥

A mad elephant, mounted by an intoxicated mahout, tramples on everything that it comes across. Likewise is a ruler devoid of the light of learning, advised by an unwise minister.

विद्याविनीतो राजा हि प्रजानां विनये रतः।
अनन्यां पृथिवीं भुङ्क्ते सर्वं भूतहिते रतः॥8॥

A ruler, disciplined by learning, will be interested in disciplining his subjects. He will enjoy the earth unopposed, devoted to the welfare of all beings.

अविश्वास्यो हि विसंवादकः स्वेषां परेषां
च भवति प्रकृतिविरुद्धाचारश्च।
तस्मात् समानशीलवेष भाषाचारतामुपगच्छेत्॥9॥

One who does not keep one's word and one whose behaviour is contrary to that of the people becomes untrustworthy to one's own people and to others. Hence (a ruler) should adopt the same mode of life, same dress, same language, and same customs as those of the people.

अनुरक्तप्रकृतिः ससहायत्वात् अल्पेनाप्य-
नुग्रहेण कार्यं साधयति॥10॥

A ruler with loyal people accomplishes his task even with a little help because of their cooperation.

सम्पादयत्यसम्पन्नाः प्रकृतीरात्मवान् नृपः।
विवृद्धाश्चानुरक्ताश्च प्रकृतीर्हन्त्यनात्मवान्॥11॥

A ruler with character can render even unendowed people happy, a characterless ruler destroys loyal and prosperous people.

नृपो हि दुष्टप्रकृतिः चातुरन्तोऽप्यनात्मवान्।
हन्यते वा प्रकृतिभिः याति वा द्विषतां वशम्॥12॥

An evil-natured and characterless ruler will be destroyed by the people or overcome by enemies.

इन्द्रयम स्थानमेतत् राजानः प्रत्यक्षहेडप्रसादाः
तानवमन्यमानं दैवोऽपि दण्डः स्पृशति॥13॥

The role of the ruler is that of Indra (the bestower of rewards) and of Yama (who metes out punishment). Rulers are that visible dispensers of (divine) punishments and rewards. Those who disrespect them will be punished by the gods.

आत्मवान् स्वल्पदेशोपि युक्तः प्रकृति सम्पदा।
न यज्ञः प्रथिवीं भुङ्क्ते जयत्येव न हीयते॥14॥

A ruler with good qualities, who knows statecraft and endowed with the wealth of loyal people, though rules a small country, yet enjoys the entire earth, ever wins and never loses.

मर्यादां स्थापयेदाचार्यान् अमात्यांश्च।
च एनंमपायस्थानेभ्यो वारयेयुः॥15॥

(A ruler) should establish right code of conduct and also appoint preceptors and ministers who will keep him off danger spots.

न धर्मार्थौ पीडयेत्॥16॥

(A ruler) should not harass the roots of righteousness and wealth.

स्वयं यच्छीलः तच्छीलाः प्रकृतयो भवन्ति॥17॥

What character the ruler himself has, the people attendant on him have.

अशास्त्रचक्षुरन्धः यत्किञ्चनकारी।
दृढाभिनिवेशी परप्रणेयो वा भवति॥18॥

The ruler blinded by not learning the various sciences acts indiscriminately, is obstinate in decisions and is led by others.

अविद्याविनयः पुरुषव्यसनहेतुः।
अविनीतो हि व्यसनदोषान् न पश्यति॥19॥

Absence of learning and discipline cause vices in men. The untrained, undisciplined and illiterate do not see the evil in vices.

कृत्स्नं हि शास्त्रमिदमिन्द्रियजयः॥20॥

The whole of learning of sciences and scriptures is this: control over the senses.

राज्ञः स्वधर्मः स्वर्गाय प्रजा धर्मेण रक्षितुः।
अरक्षितुर्वा क्षेप्रुर्वा मिथ्यादण्डमतोऽन्यथा॥21॥

A ruler who performs his duty righteously and protects his people properly goes to heaven. Quite contrary is the case with one who does not protect his people or metes out unjust punishment.

चातुर्वर्णाश्रमस्यायं लोकस्याचाररक्षणात्।
नश्चतां सर्वधर्माणां राजा धर्मप्रवर्तकः॥22॥

By enforcing the adherence of the people to the observance of duties prescribed for the four castes and the four stages of life and rooting out all unrighteousness the ruler functions as the dispenser of justice.

अनुशासद्धि धर्मेण व्यवहारेण संस्थया।
न्यायेन च चतुर्थेन चतुरन्तां महीं जयेत्॥23॥

A ruler who administers justice on the basis of four principles: righteousness, evidence, history of the case and the prevalent law shall conquer the four corners of the earth.

धर्मो ह्यधर्मोपहतः शास्तारं हन्त्युपेक्षितः॥24॥

Righteousness, overcome by unrighteousness, destroys the ruler, if neglect is shown.

जित्वा च पृथिवीं विभक्तवर्णाश्रमां स्वधर्मेण
भुञ्जीत॥25॥

After conquering the earth consisting of diverse groups of people in various stages of life, the ruler should enjoy it, governing according to prescribed duties.

यथा चण्डालोदपानः चण्डालानमेवोपभोग्यः नान्येषां।
एवमय राजा नीचानामेवोपभोग्यः नार्याणाम्॥30॥

Just as the well belonging to (outcaste) huntsmen is of use only to them and not to others, so this (depraved) ruler is of use only to low type of people and not to men of noble character.

दूतमुखा वै राजानः, तस्मादुद्धृतेष्वपि
शस्त्रेषु यथोक्तं वक्तारः! तेषामन्तावसायिनो-
ऽप्यवध्याः, किमङ्ग! पुनर्ब्राह्मणाः?॥31॥

Envoys are the mouthpieces of rulers. Hence even if weapons are raised they speak as they have been told to speak. Of these even the low born are immune from killing. What to speak of Brahmins?

अपराधं सहेताल्पं तृप्येदल्पेऽपि चोदये॥32॥

The ruler should condone minor offences and be satisfied even when the revenue is small.

प्रत्यक्षपरोक्षानुमेया हि राजवृत्तिः॥33॥

A ruler's actions are based on what is patently seen, what is not directly seen and what has to be inferred.

दुर्दशो हि राजा कार्याकार्यविपर्या समासन्नैः कार्यते॥34॥

An inaccessible ruler is made to do the opposite of what ought or ought not to be done by those surrounding him.

सर्वमात्ययिकं कार्यं श्रृणुयान्नातिपातयेत्।
कृच्छ्रसाध्यमतिक्रान्तमसाध्यं वा विजायते॥35॥

(A ruler) should attend to all urgent matters promptly and never postpone them. A matter, deferred consideration and decision, becomes more difficult or impossible to tackle.

2. Counsellors, Aides, Allies

सहायसाध्यं राजत्वं चक्रमेकं न वर्तते।
कुर्वीत सचिवांस्तस्मात् तेषां च श्रृणुयान्मतम्॥36॥

Governance is possible only with assistance. A single wheel does not move. Hence ministers should be appointed and their counsel listened to.

मन्त्रशक्तिहीनः प्राज्ञपुरुषोपचयं विद्यावृद्धिसंयोगं वा कुर्वीत। तथा हि सद्यः श्रेयः प्राप्नोति॥37॥

(The ruler) devoid of the power of counsel should gather around him a collection of wise men or consult learned elders. Thus would he attain immediate prosperity.

इन्द्रस्य हि मन्त्रिपरिषदृषीणां सहस्रं,
स तच्चक्षुः तस्मादिमं द्वयक्षं सहस्राक्षमाहुः॥38॥

Indra's council of ministers consists of one thousand sages. That is his eye. Hence it is that they call him "the thousand-eyed one", though he has only two eyes.

प्रियो यस्य भवेद्यो वा प्रियोऽस्य कतरस्तयोः?
प्रियो यस्य स तं गच्छेत् इत्याश्रयगतिः परा॥39॥

(With whom shall an alliance be made?): one to whom he is dear or one who is dear to him? He shall go to him, to whom he is dear. This is the best way of forming an alliance.

अभ्युच्चितश्चाविश्वास्यः, 'ऋद्धिर्हि चित्तविकारिणी॥40॥

An ally with increased power is untrustworthy, for prosperity changes the mind.

आपद्धि सौहृदस्थैर्यमुत्पादयति॥41॥

Difficulties stabilise friendships.

उपकारलक्षणं मित्रम्॥42॥

Rendering help is the sign of a friend.

सगन्धा ह्येनमपचरन्तमपि न त्यजन्ति॥43॥

Those with established relationship do not desert, even if offended.

अमानुषेण्वपि चैतदृश्यते गावो ह्यसगन्धं
गोगणमतिक्रम्य सगन्धेण्वे वावतिष्ठन्ते इति॥44॥

Such loyalty is seen even among animals. For example, cows pass by unaccustomed herds and stay always in the company of known herds.

सगन्धा ह्यस्य सर्वमवगृह्य स्वामिवत्प्रचरन्ति॥45॥

Those whose relationship with the ruler is established over a long period are however likely to completely take over everything from the ruler and pose as rulers themselves.

सहाध्यायिनः विश्वास्या अपि सह
क्रीडितत्वात, परिभवन्ति॥46॥

Classmates, though they are trustworthy, will not respect the ruler, having been playmates. Hence they should not be appointed as ministers.

गुह्यसधर्माणो हि समानशीलव्यसनत्वा-
न्यर्मज्ञभयान्नापराध्यन्ति॥47॥

Those who have a similar nature in secret matters and who have common vices and habits (in common with the ruler) do not offend him out of fear that he knows their secrets.

यथा ह्यश्रोत्रियः श्राद्धं न सतां भोक्तुमर्हति।
एवमश्रुतशास्त्रार्थः न मन्त्रं श्रोतुमर्हति॥48॥

Just as those not well-versed in the scriptures are unfit to eat the feast offerings to the dead given by good people, so too rulers not well-versed in the various sciences of state are not fit to hear ministerial counsel.

विशिष्टादल्पमप्यंशं लब्ध्वा तुष्टमुखो व्रजेत्॥49॥

(A weak ally) even if he gets only a small share or the spoils of victory from the superior ally should appear contented.

आलम्वनाभावे ह्यालम्बिता न विद्यते॥50॥

In the absence of support, the supported do not exist.

3. Policy towards Enemies

वितंसगिलवत् विश्वासेनामिपेण चारीन् हन्यात्॥51॥

As a bird is captured by a bait in the form of a bird, enemies should be destroyed by creating trust and offering a bait.

नार्हत्यात्मक्षयेण मित्रमुखानमित्रान् वर्धयितुम्॥52॥

One should not allow enemies posing as friends to grow at one's expense.

वैरिणा सह विश्वासं यो नरः कर्तुमिच्छति।
स वृक्षाग्रेषु संसुप्तः पतितः प्रतिबुध्यते॥115॥

He who wishes to trust the enemy is deemed as the one who slept on the tips of tree branches and fell.

न विश्वसेत् पूर्वपराजितस्य शत्रोश्च मित्रत्वमुपागतस्य।
दग्धां गुहां पश्यत घूकपूर्णां काक प्रणीतेन
हुताशनेन॥116॥

An enemy who was defeated earlier and who has since become a friend should not be trusted, as a burnt cave filled with smoke is not trusted by the crow, even after the fire is extinguished.

न विश्वसेत् कुमित्रे च मित्रे चापि न विश्वसेत्।
कदाचित् कुपितं मित्रं सर्व गुह्यं प्रकाशयेत्॥117॥

One should not trust a bad friend or even a good friend. Sometimes an angered friend discloses all secrets.

यत् प्रसह्य हरेदन्यः तत् प्रयच्छेदुपायतः॥53॥

One should offer (to one enemy) that which is likely to be taken by force by another enemy.

हस्तिप्रधानो हि परानीकवधः॥54॥

Destruction of enemy's army is primarily the destruction of their elephants.

जायते प्लक्षबीजाशात् कपोतादिव शाल्मलेः।
उद्वेगजननो नित्यं पश्चादपि भयावहः॥55॥

Just as a pigeon which has lived on the holy fig tree (plaksha) is a source of constant danger to the silk cotton tree (salmali) so (a person who has come after living with an enemy) is a source of constant danger.

4. Military Policy

अनेकमुख्यं हि परस्परभयात् परोपजापं नोपैति॥56॥

Armed forces under several commands do not, due to mutual fear, go over to the enemy.

एकस्था हि शस्त्रग्रहणसमर्थाः स्युः॥57॥

(Groups of people) if stationed at one place are capable of acquiring arms.

हस्तिप्रधानो हि विजयो राज्ञाम्॥58॥

Victory of rulers in battle depends mainly on elephants.

समेन च आमं पात्रमामेनाहतमिव उभयतः क्षयं करोति॥59॥

A fight between equals, like the collision of one unbaked pot with another, destroys both.

कुम्भेनेवाश्मा हीनेनैकान्तसिद्धिमवाप्नोति॥60॥

In a fight with an inferior, one attains absolute victory, like the stone hitting an earthen pot.

तेजो हि सन्धानकारणम्। नातप्त लोहं लोहेन सन्ध
ीयते॥61॥

Power is the cause for the forging of treaties. Unheated metal does not join with metal.

पुनरावर्तमानस्य निराशस्य च जीविते।
अधार्यो जायते वेगः तस्माद्भग्नं न पीडयेत्॥62॥

The force of (an army) which returns to fight, without any desire to live, is irresistible. Hence a broken army should not be harassed.

दिवा काकः कौशिकं हन्ति
रात्रौ कौशिकः काकम्॥63॥

In day time the crow kills the owl. At night the owl kills the crow. (The time of fight is important.)

श्वराहयोः कलहे अन्यतरसिद्धिश्चण्डालस्य॥64॥

In the fight between the dog and the pig the ultimate victory is that of the pariah (who gets the meat to eat).

स्थलगतो हि श्वा नक्रं विकर्षति।
निम्नगतो नक्रः श्वानम्॥65॥

A dog on land drags a crocodile. A crocodile in water drags a dog. (The place of fight is important.)

समज्यायेभ्यां सन्धीयेत, हीनेन विगृह्लीयात्॥66॥

One should sign a treaty of peace with one's equal and superior and fight with the inferior.

विगृहीतो हि ज्यायसा हस्तिना पादयुद्धमिवाभ्युपैति॥67॥

Fighting a superior is like an infantry soldier fighting an elephant.

सर्वत्रानुप्रणतो हि कुलैडक इव निराशो
जीविते वसति। युद्धयमानश्चाल्पसैन्य:
समुद्रमिवाप्लवोऽवगाहमान: सीदति।
तद्विशिष्टं तु राजानमाश्रिती दुर्गमविपह्यं
वा चेष्टेत॥68॥

(A weak ruler) surrendering to everyone lives without hope in life like the crab on the river bank (always in the danger of being captured). One who fights with a small army perishes like the one who tries to cross the sea without a boat. Hence he should seek refuge with a powerful ruler or remain in an impregnable fort.

अवश्यमपि हि शक्यं सामादिमिर्वश्यं कर्तुम्॥69॥

An army not under control can be brought under control by conciliation and other means.

5. Financial Policy

आकार प्रभव: कोश:॥70॥

The treasury has its source in the mines.

कोशाद्दण्ड: प्रजायते॥71॥

From (the strength of) the treasury the army is born.

पृथिवी कोशदण्डाभ्य प्राप्यते कोशभूषणा॥72॥

Through the treasury and the army, the earth, whose adornment is the treasury, is obtained.

अर्थ एव प्रधान इति कौटल्य:
अर्थमूलौ हि धर्मकामाविति॥73॥

Material wealth alone is importnat, says Kautilya, for, both righteousness and pleasure are based on material wealth.

जित्वाऽपि हि क्षीणदण्डकोशः पराजितो भवति॥74॥

Even after winning (a battle) a ruler with a weak army and treasury is a loser.

अनुत्थाने ध्रुवो नाशः प्राप्तस्यानागतस्य च।
प्राप्यते फलमुत्थानाल्लभते चार्थसम्पदम्॥75॥

In inactivity there is certain destruction (sure loss) of what has been achieved and of what is to come.

By activity, objectives are achieved and abundance of wealth acquired.

अर्थो धर्म कामः इति अर्थत्रिवगंः।
तस्य पूर्वः पूर्वः श्रेयानुपसंप्राप्तुम्॥76॥

Riches, righteousness and physical pleasures – these are the three kinds of wealth. It is preferable to first attain the earlier mentioned ones than the latter.

अनर्थोऽधर्मः शोक इति अनर्थत्रिवर्गः।
तस्य पूर्वः पूर्वः श्रेयान् प्रति कर्तुम्॥77॥

Absence of riches, absence of righteousness and absence of enjoyment are the three kinds of poverty. It is preferable to counteract the ones mentioned earlier first than the latter.

कोशपूर्वाः सर्वारम्भा॥78॥

The launching of all programmes depends first and foremost on the (resources of the) treasury.

धर्ममूलत्वात् कामफलत्वाच्चार्थस्य
धर्मामंकामानुबन्धा या अर्थस्य सिद्धिः
सा सर्वार्थ सिद्धिः॥79॥

Since righteousness is the root of wealth and enjoyment fruit, attainment of wealth linked to righteousness and enjoyment is attainment of all riches.

अल्पकोशो हि राजा पौरजानपदानेव ग्रसते।।80।।

A ruler with a depleted treasury will devour the citizens of cities and the people of villages.

नाधनाः प्राप्नुवन्त्यर्थान् नरा यत्नशतैरपि।
अर्थैरर्थाः प्रबध्यन्ते गजाः प्रतिगजैरिव।।81।।

Men without wealth do not attain their objectives even after hundreds of trials.

Only through wealth can material gains be attained as elephants (wild) can be captured only when tamed.

क्षीण निचयं चावाप्तमपि।
राज्यं क्षया चैव भवति।।82।।

A state with depleted resources, even if acquired, becomes only a liability.

पक्वं पक्वमिवारामात् फलं राज्यादवाप्नुयात्,
आत्मच्छेदभयादामं वर्जयेत् कोपकारकं।।83।।

Just as only ripe fruits are collected from a garden, so too the fruits of the state (revenue) should be collected only when due. Collection of unripe fruits (premature collection of revenue) should be avoided as this will generate the wrath of the people and result in self-destruction.

6. Corruption

यथा ह्यनास्वादयितुं न शक्यं जिह्वातलस्थं
मधु वा विषं वा। अर्थस्तथा ह्यर्थचरेण
राज्ञः स्वल्पोऽप्यनास्वादयितुं न शक्यः।।84।।

Just as it is difficult not to taste honey or poison

placed on the tongue, similarly, it is difficult for one handling the ruler's money to refrain from tasting it in at least small quantities.

मत्स्याः यथाऽन्तस्सलिले चरन्तो ज्ञातुं न
शक्याः सलिलं पिबन्तः। युक्तास्तथा कार्यविधौ
नियुक्ताः ज्ञातुं न शक्या धनमाददानाः॥85॥

Just as it is not possible to know when the fish moving in water drink water, similarly, it is difficult to find out when officers employed in the execution of works misappropriate money.

अपि शक्या गतिर्ज्ञातुं पततां रवेपतत्रिणाम्।
न तु प्रच्छन्नभावानां युक्तानां चरतां गतिः॥86॥

Even the path of birds flying in the sky can be found out but not the ways of officers who hide their intentions.

दृश्यते ह्यचोरोऽपि चोरमार्गे यदृच्छया
सन्निपातेन चोरवेषशस्त्रभाण्डसामान्येन
च गुह्यमाणः, चोरभाण्डस्योपवासेन वा॥87॥

Even one who is not a thief is likely to be captured as a thief, if he is seen accidentally on the scene of theft, or if there is resemblance between the dress, weapons and other articles of the thief and his, or if he is seen near the stolen articles.

क्षीरघृतभृता हि वत्सानुपहन्युः॥88॥

(The cowherds) if given wages in the form of milk and ghee act to the detriment of calves.

यः समुदयं परिहापयति स राजार्थं भक्षयति॥89॥

He who is responsible for loss of revenue shall be deemed to have eaten the ruler's property.

यः समुदयं द्विगुणभुद्भावयति स जनपदं भक्षयति॥90॥

He who doubles the revenue eats up the people's property.

यः समुदयं व्ययमुपनयति स पुरुषकर्माणि भक्षयति॥91॥

He who causes expenditure equal to the revenue eats up the labour of workmen.

न दूषणमदुष्टस्य विषेणवाम्भसश्चरेत्।
कदाचिद्धि प्रदुष्टस्य नाधिगम्येत भेषजम्॥92॥

The pure shall not be corrupted, as water by poison. Sometimes it may not be possible to find a cure for the corrupted.

कृता च कलुषा बुद्धिः नागत्वान्तं
निवर्तेत स्थिता सत्ववतां धृतौ॥93॥

The intellect of the brave, trained to be steadfast, once corrupted may not return without reaching the end (the summit of corruption).

महत्यर्थापहारे अल्पेनापि सिद्धः सर्वं भजेत॥94॥

In a case of misappropriation involving a large amount of money if a government servant is proved to be guilty of even a small part he shall be held liable for the whole amount.

7. Guarding of Secrets

यावद्भयो गुह्यमाचष्टे नरेभ्यः पुरुषाधिपः
अवशः कर्मणा तेन वश्यो भवति तावताम्॥95॥

To as many men a ruler divulges a secret, on so many he becomes dependent, rendered helpless by that act of his.

असंवृतस्य कार्याणि प्राप्तान्यपि विशेषतः।
निस्संशयं विपद्यन्ते भिन्नप्लव इवोदधौ॥96॥

The tasks of one whose secrets are not kept even if accomplished with special success will undoubtedly get ruined like the broken vessel on the sea.

प्रमादमदसुप्तप्रलापकामादिरुत्सेकः
प्रच्छन्नोऽवमतो वा मन्त्रं भिनत्ति॥97॥

A person under the influence of carelessness, intoxication, or prattling while asleep or enjoying carnal pleasures, or one hidden or dishonoured discloses secret counsel.

मन्त्रभेदो ह्ययोगक्षेमकरः राज्ञः तदायत्तपुरुषाणां च॥98॥

The disclosure of secret counsel is injurious to the welfare of the ruler and his staff.

कामद्वेषहर्षदन्यव्रूवसायभयद्वन्द्वविपर्यासं
इङ्गिताकाराभ्यां हि मन्त्रसंवरणार्थमावरन्ति प्राज्ञाः॥99॥

Wise men exhibit in their gestures and expressions the opposite of their feeling in the pairs: love and hatred, pleasure and sorrow, determination and fear etc. in order to hide their secrets.

8. Law, Justice, Punishment

सर्वेषामपि हि स्त्रीदायाद्यदोषः कर्मस्पर्धा
प्रतिपक्षद्वेषः पण्यसंस्था समवायो वा विवादपदाना-
मन्यतमं वा रोषस्थानं रोषनिमित्तो घातः॥100॥

In all cases an offence concerning women or relatives, professional rivalry, hatred of opposition, market association, or trade guilds, any of the legal disputes, the origin is anger. Anger results in murder.

धर्मश्च व्यवहारश्च चरित्रं राजशासनम्।
विवादार्थश्चतुष्पादः पश्चिमः पूर्वबाधकः॥101॥

A case in dispute is four-legged. It depends on: (1) what is right according to ethical principles, (2) evidence, (3) custom and (4) the ruler's order. The last one overrules all the earlier ones.

अत्र सत्ये स्थितो धर्मः व्यवहारस्तु साक्षिष।
चरित्रं संग्रहे पुंसां राज्ञामाज्ञा तु शासनम्॥102॥

What is right is based on truth, evidence on witnesses, custom on available tradition of the people and the law is the ruler's command.

संस्थया धर्मशास्त्रेण शास्त्रं वा व्यावहारिकम्।
यस्मिन्नर्थे विरुद्धयेत धर्मेणार्थं विनिश्चयेत्॥103॥

When there is conflict between established tradition and ethical principles or between evidence and what is right (according to ethical principles) the case shall be decided on the basis of ethical principles.

शास्त्रं विप्रतिपद्येत धर्मन्यायेन केनचित्।
न्यायस्तत्र प्रमाणं स्यात् तत्र पाठो हि नश्यति॥104॥

Where scriptural laws conflict with what is righteous and just, there justice shall be the valid criterion, the written text loses its relevance.

धर्ममर्थं चोपदिशेत् नाधर्मं अनर्थं च॥105॥

Only that should be taught which conduces to righteousness and material prosperity and not what leads to unrighteousness and material disaster.

तीक्ष्ण दण्डो हि भूतानामुद्वेजनीयः,
मृदुदण्डः परिभूयते, यथार्हदण्डः पूज्यः॥106॥

He who punishes severely is hated by the people, he who punishes mildly is despised, one who metes out deserving punishment is respected.

सुविज्ञातप्रणीतो हि दण्डः प्रजाः धर्मार्थमैर्योजयति॥107॥

Punishment meted out after due consideration keeps the people attached to righteousness and to tasks conducive to material wealth and enjoyment.

दुष्प्रणीतस्तु कामक्रोधभ्यामज्ञानाद्वानप्रस्थ-
परिव्राजकानपि कोपयति, किमङ्ग! पुनः गृहस्थान्?॥108॥

Wrong punishment meted out in anger, lust or ignorance angers even sages of the forest. What to speak of householders?

अप्रणीतो हि दण्डः मात्स्यन्यायमुद्भावयति॥109॥

If no punishment is given, the law of the fishes (strong swallowing the weak) is created.

बलीयानबलं हि ग्रसते दण्डधराभावे॥110॥

In the absence of punishment, the strong swallows the weak.

चतुवर्णाश्रमो लोको राज्ञा दण्डेन पालितः।
स्वधर्मकर्माभिरतो वर्तते स्वेषु वर्त्मसु (वेश्मसु)॥111॥

The people of the four genres and the four stages of life function in their respective spheres, when ruled by the ruler with appropriate punishment.

विनयमूलो दण्डः प्राणभृतां योगक्षेमावहः॥112॥

Punishment, the root of discipline, is the source of prosperity for the people.

नवास्तु यमस्थाने दण्डधरं मन्यमानाः नापराध्यन्ति॥113॥

New men deeming the dispenser of punishment as Yama incarnate do not commit crimes.

दण्डकरा हि राजानः प्रजानां किल्बिष
हरन्ति, योगक्षेमवहाश्च भवन्ति॥114॥

Rulers armed with the staff of punishment remove people's miseries and bring about their security and welfare.

दोषशुद्धौ हि दूष्या न विद्यन्ते॥115॥

When guilt is removed there are no guilty men.

दूष्यशुद्धौ हि दोषः पुनरन्यान् दूषयति॥116॥

When guilty men are removed, the guilt will again contaminate others.

समाः सर्वेषु भावेषु विश्वास्याः लोक संप्रियाः॥117॥

(Judges) should be impartial to all beings, trustworthy, and liked by the people.

दण्डो हि केवलं लोकं परं चेमं च रक्षति।
राज्ञा पुत्रे च शत्रौ च यथादोष समं धृतः॥118॥

Punishment, meted out by the ruler according to offence equally, (without discrimination) to sons and enemies alike, protects alone this world and the other.

सर्वापराधेष्वपीडनीयो हि ब्राह्मणः॥119॥

Whatever be the crime the learned one should not be tortured.

न चाभि युक्तेऽभियोगोऽस्ति॥120॥

Against an accused there can be no other suit.

कृतकार्यविनिश्चयो ह्यभियोक्ता, नाभियुक्तः॥121॥

It is the prosecutor who decides what is to be done, not the accused.

ध्रुवं हि साक्षिभिः श्रोतव्यम्॥122॥

Truth has to be spoken by witnesses.

असारं हि बालप्रातिभाव्यम्॥123॥

The guarantee of a minor has no value.

अनीश्वरा हि पितृमन्तः पुत्राः॥124॥

Sons having fathers (alive) have no right to property.

विवाहपूर्वो हि व्यवहारः॥125॥

Marriage precedes disputes.

अमोक्षो हि धर्मविवाहानाम्॥126॥

Righteous marriages are indissoluble.

तीर्थोपरोधो हि धर्म वधः॥127॥

Denial of sexual pleasure to a wife, after her monthly ablution (periods) is a transgression of (the husband's) duty.

आपदर्थ हि स्त्रीधनम्॥128॥

It is to meet unforeseen difficulties that a woman is given property (dowry) (at the time of marriage).

9. Causes of People's Discontent

अप्रदानैश्च देयानां अदेयानां च साधनैः॥129॥

By not giving donations which ought to be given and accepting donations which should not be taken.

अदण्डनैश्च दण्ड्यानां अदण्ड्यानां चण्डदण्डनैः॥130॥

By not punishing the guilty and severely punishing the innocent.

अग्राह्याणामुपग्राहैः ग्राह्याणां चानभिग्रहैः॥131॥

By arresting those who should not be arrested and not arresting those deserving to be arrested.

उचितानां चरित्राणां धर्मिष्ठानां निवर्तनैः॥132॥

By the stoppage of righteous and appropriate customs.

अधर्मस्य प्रसङ्गेन धर्म स्यावग्रहेण च॥133॥

By the encouragement of unrighteousness and the discouragement of righteousness.

अकार्याणां च करणैः कार्याणां च प्रणाशनैः॥134॥

By doing what ought not to be done and preventing what ought to be done.

उपघातैः प्रधानानां मान्यानां चावमाननैः॥135॥

By harming important leaders of the people and dishonouring respectable ones.

सर्वस्वनाशे संजाते प्राणानामपि संशये।
अपि शत्रुं प्रणम्योच्चै रक्षेत् प्राणान् धनानि च॥134॥

When the loss of one's wealth and danger to life is imminent, (the ruler) should bow before the enemy and protect his life and wealth.

10. Formation of Alliances

कालेन रिपुणा सन्धिः काले मित्रेण विग्रहः।
कार्यकारणमाश्रित्य कालं क्षिपति पण्डितः॥135॥

In proper time alliance should be made with enemies and war fought with friends. The wise one lets go time with a purpose and to achieve the task.

व्यसने सति कुर्वीत येन केनापि संगतिम्।
ऋक्षवानर गोपुच्छैः पुरा दाशरथिर्यथा॥141॥

When in difficulty, the ruler should conclude an alliance with anyone available, as Rama did in olden days, with bears, monkeys etc. (animals with tails).

सुकुले योजयेत् कन्यां पुत्रं विद्यासु योजयेत्।
व्यसने योजयेच्छत्रुमिष्टं धर्मेण योजयेत्॥130॥

The enemy should be linked to difficulties, the daughter to a good family, son to education, and a friend to righteous path.

वहेदमित्रं स्कन्धेन यावत् काल विपर्ययः।
तथैवमागते काले भिन्द्याद् घटमिवाश्मनि॥136॥

The enemy should be carried on one's shoulders so long as the times are adverse, but should be attacked when the proper time comes, as the earthen pot with a stone.

नात्मच्छिद्रं परो विद्याद् विद्याच्छिद्रं परस्य तु।
गूहेत् कूर्म इवाङ्गानि परभावं च लक्षयेत्॥137॥

The enemy should not know one's own weakness, but one should know the enemy's weakness. One should hide one's intention, as the tortoise withdraws its limbs, and watch the enemy's posture.

विरोधनैश्च वृद्धानां वैषम्येणानृतेन च॥136॥

By estrangement of elders, by nepotism and falsehood.

कृतस्याप्रतिकारेण स्थितस्याकरणेन च॥137॥

By not repaying for what was done (in help) and not doing what was agreed to be done.

अनर्थ्यानां च करणैः अर्थ्यानां च विघातनैः॥138॥

By undertaking schemes which result in loss and stopping those which would result in gain.

अरक्षणैश्च चोरेभ्यः स्वयं च परिपोषणैः॥139॥

By not protecting the people from thieves and robbers and enriching himself at their cost.

पातैः पुरुषकाराणां कर्मणां गुणदूषणैः॥140॥

By preventing manly endeavour and criticising good work.

अवक्षेपेण हि सतां असतां प्रग्रहेण च॥141॥

By the disrespect shown to the good ones and the encouragement of the unrighteous.

अभूतानां च हिंसानामधर्माणां प्रवर्तनैः॥142॥

By acts of unprecedented and unrighteous violence.

उचितानां चरित्राणां धर्मिष्टानां निवर्तनै।
अधर्मस्य प्रसङ्गेन धर्मस्यावग्रहेण च
प्रकृतीनां क्षयो लोभः वैराग्यं वोपजायते॥143॥

By the stoppage of righteous and appropriate customs, by the encouragement of unrighteousness and disregard of righteousness, decadence, avarice, and disaffection are generated in the people.

राज्ञः प्रमादालस्याभ्यां योगक्षेमवधेन च॥144॥

By the destruction of the security and welfare of the people due to the negligence and laziness of the ruler.

प्रकृतीनां क्षयो लोभः वैराग्यं चोपजायते॥145॥

Impoverishment, avarice and discontent are produced in the people.

क्षीणाः प्रकृतयो लोभं लुब्धा यान्ति वरागताम्॥146॥

Impoverished people become avaricious and avaricious people become discontented.

विरक्ता यान्त्यमित्रं वा भर्तारं ध्नन्ति वा स्वयम्॥147॥

Discontented people go over to the enemy or destroy the rulers themselves.

11. Ruling Family, Ruling Class

ब्राह्मणेनैधितः क्षत्रं मन्त्रिमन्त्राभिमन्त्रितम्।
जयत्यजितमत्यन्तं शास्त्रानुगमशस्त्रितम्॥148॥

The power of the ruling class, augmented by the learned preceptor, buttressed by the counsel of good ministers, armed with the compliance of scriptures and sciences triumphs and ever remains unvanquished.

सङ्घाः हि संहतत्वादधृष्याः परेषाम्॥149॥

Corporations (or groups of exclusive ruling class) being close-knit are not easily assailable by enemies.

काष्ठमिव हि घुणजग्धं राजकुलं
अविनीतमभियुक्तमात्रं भज्यते॥150॥

A ruling family composed of indisciplined and dissolute members breaks like moth-eaten wood.

12. Duties of Officials

लोक यात्रावित् राजानमात्मद्रव्यप्रकृतिसम्पन्नं
प्रियहितद्वारेणाश्रयेत॥151॥

A worldly wise person should seek, through the agency of a dear friend, the service of a ruler endowed with personal qualities, wealth and loyal subjects.

द्रव्यप्रकृतिहीनमप्याश्रयेत, न त्वेवानात्मसम्पन्नम्।
अनात्मवान् हि नीतिशास्त्र विद्वेषादनर्थ्यसंयोगद्वा
प्राप्यापि महदैश्वर्यं न भवति॥152॥

One may seek to serve a ruler devoid of wealth or loyal subjects, but never a ruler without character, for a characterless ruler disregards the tenets of political science, associates himself with evil company and comes to ruin even after inheriting a large and prosperous kingdom.

एकदेशं दहेदग्निः शरीरं वा परं गतः।
सपुत्रदार राजा तु घातयेद्वर्धयेत वा॥153॥

Fire may burn a part or whole of the body. But a ruler can destroy one along with his wife and children. He can also cause their advancement.

अविसंवादाद्धि स्थानस्थैर्यमवाप्नोति॥154॥

Absence of a contradicting tendency makes one's position secure.

अहीनकालं राजार्थं स्वार्थं प्रियहितैस्सह।
परार्थं देशकाले च ब्रूयाद्धर्मार्थसंहितम्॥155॥

(A courtier) should speak out the ruler's interest without loss of time, his own interest with his dear friends, others' interests at the appropriate time and place, keeping in view the requirements of righteousness and material well-being.

मतिकर्मसु पृष्टो हि तदात्वे आयत्यां च धर्मार्थसंयुक्तं।
समर्थं प्रवीणवत् अपरिषद्भीरुः कथयेत्॥156॥

(A courtier) when questioned by a ruler on important matters requiring intellectual analysis, should, like an expert and unafraid of the assembly, mention his views on what is practicable, consistent with righteousness and material benefit.

मित्रमुखा ह्यमित्रास्ते, ये साहसमधर्म-
मर्थातिक्रमं च ग्राह्यन्ति॥157॥

Those who goad one into rash acts, unrighteousness and extravagance are really enemies under the mask of friends.

परात् संक्रामयेत् घोरं न च घोरं स्वयं वदेत्॥158॥

One should avoid hearing evil aspersions spoken about others nor speak such things oneself.

तितिक्षेतात्मनश्चैव क्षमावान् पृथिवीसमः॥159॥

One should forgive evil words spoken to oneself and have forbearance like that of the earth.

अप्रिया अपि दक्षास्स्युः तद्भावाद्ये वहिष्कृताः॥160॥

Even competent persons speaking unpleasant things have been banished by rulers.

अनर्थ्याश्च प्रिया दृष्टाः चित्तज्ञानानुवर्तिनः॥161॥

Undesirable persons become favourites by acting according to the reading of the ruler's mind.

अभिहास्येष्वभिहसेत् घोरहासांश्च वर्जयेत्॥162॥

One may laugh at jokes, but never laugh loudly.

आत्मरक्षा हि सततं पूर्वं कार्या विजानता।
अग्नाविव हि संप्रोक्ता वृत्ती राजोपजीविनाम्॥163॥

The wise ones should always first look to their own self-protection. Those who serve rulers are said to function in fire.

पुष्टः प्रियहितं ब्रूयात् न ब्रूयादहितं प्रियम्॥164॥

When asked, one should speak out what is pleasing and beneficial. One should not speak pleasing things which are not beneficial.

अप्रियं वा हितं ब्रूयात् शृण्वतोऽनुसतो मिथः॥166॥

What is good, though unpleasant, shall be spoken in private, if (the listener) is willing to listen.

तूष्णीं वा प्रतिवाक्ये स्यात् द्वेष्यादींश्च न वर्णयेत्॥167॥

One may even be silent in reply but never mention anything displeasing.

कृतप्रणाशः शक्तिहानिः विद्यापण्यत्वं आशुनिर्वेदः
देशलौल्यं अविश्वासः बलवद्विग्रहो वा
परित्यागस्थानम्॥168॥

The occasions when one should leave one's post are: (a) when one's work gets destroyed without fruition, (b) one's power gets reduced, (c) when one's learning is treated like a tradeable commodity, (d) one's hopes are frustrated, (e) one is eager to be in new countries, (f) when one loses the confidence of the master, (g) when one comes into conflict with powerful people.

From Chanakyarajanitisastram

॥ श्रीः ॥

चाणक्यराजनीतिशास्त्रम्

1. Duties and Qualities of the Ruler

लिङ्गपूजन धर्मात्मा गोब्राह्मणहिते रतः
प्रजाः पालयितुं शक्तः स राजा यो जितेन्द्रियः॥1॥

The ruler who has controlled his senses, is religious, venerates ascetics, is righteous and interested in the welfare of his subjects is competent to protect his people.

स्वं राष्ट्रं पालयेन्जित्यं सत्यधर्मपरायणः
निर्जित्य पर सैन्यानि क्षितिं धर्मेण पालयेत्॥2॥

The ruler shall rule his country, devoted to truth and righteousness, and defeating enemy forces, righteously protect his territory.

ओंकारशब्दो विप्राणां यस्य राष्ट्रे प्रवर्तते
स राजा हि भवेद् योगी व्याधिभिश्च न पीड़यते॥3॥

The ruler, in whose country the pranava sound, "om", chanted by the learned flourishes, becomes skilful and free from affliction.

अनाथानां नायो गतिरंगतिकानां व्यसनिनां
विनेता भीतानामभयमधतीनां भर वशः
सुहृद् बन्धुः स्वामी शरणमुपकारी वर गुरुः
पिता माता भ्राता जगति पुरुषो यः स नृपतिः॥4॥

He is the ruler who is the protector of the orphaned, refuge of the refugees, guide to the afflicted, protector of the frightened, the support of the unsteady, the friend, the relative, the master, the benefactor, the teacher, father, mother, brother to all.

प्रभूतं कार्यमल्पं वा यो नरः कर्तुमिच्छति।
सर्वारम्भेण तत् कुर्यात् सिंहादेकं प्रचक्षते।।8।।

One should learn from the lion to undertake a task well-prepared whether it is a big one or small.

इन्द्रियाणि च संयम्य बकवत् पण्डितो नरः।
देशकालबलं ज्ञात्वा सर्वकार्याणि साधयेत्।।9।।

Like a crane, the learned one should control his senses and knowing the aptness of time and place, accomplish all tasks.

प्रत्युत्थानं च युद्धं च संविभाग च बन्धुषु।
स्व्यमाक्रम्य भुञ्जीत शिक्षेच्चत्वारि कुक्कुटात।।10।।

From the cock one should learn four things: getting up in time, fighting, division of responsibility among allies and enjoyment after attacking oneself.

गूढ़मैधुनधाष्टर्य च काले काले च संग्रहम्।
अप्रमादमविश्वासं पञ्च शिक्षेच्च वायसात्।।11।।

From the crow one should learn five things: sex in secrecy, secret action, catch in time, unruffled behaviour and distrust of everyone.

वह्वाशी स्वल्पसंतुष्टः सुनिद्रो लघु चेतनः।
स्वामिभक्तश्च शूरश्चच षडते श्वानतो गुणाः।।12।।

These are the six qualities of the dog: desire for much, satisfaction with a little, deep slumber, quick awakening, devotion to master and bravery.

दुष्टस्य दण्डः सुजनस्य पूजा
न्यायेन कोशस्य विवर्धनं च।
अपक्षपातोऽर्थिषु राज्यरक्षा
पञ्चैव यज्ञाः कथिता नृपाणाम्॥5॥

The ruler's duties are stated to be five: punishment of the wicked, rewarding the righteous, development of state revenues by just means, impartiality in granting favours and protection of the state.

पात्रे त्यागी गुणो रागी भोगी परिजनैः सह।
शास्त्रे बोद्धा रणे योद्धा नृपतेः पञ्चलक्षणम्॥6॥

The characteristics of a ruler are five: he gives up wealth in favour of the needy, loves virtues, enjoys pleasures in the company of friends and relatives, is anxious to learn the sciences and is a fighter in war.

सिंहादेकं बकादेकं शिक्षेच्चत्वारि कुक्कुटात्।
वायसात् पञ्च शिक्षेच्च षट् शुनस्त्रीणि गर्दभात्॥7॥

The ruler should learn one quality each from the lion and the crane, four from the cock, five from the crow, six from the dog and three from the donkey.

सुश्रान्तोपि बहेद् भारं शीतोष्णं न च पश्यति।
सन्तुष्टश्चरते नित्यं त्रीणि शिक्षेच्च गर्दभात्॥13॥

From the donkey three things should be learnt: to carry the burden even though tired, not to mind heat or cold and to trudge ever satisfied.

विंशदेते गुणाः प्रोक्ता यस्तु कुर्याद् विचक्षणः।
स जेष्यति रिपून् सर्वात् जेयश्च न भविष्यति॥14॥

The discerning one who practises these twenty virtues mentioned conquers all enemies and himself remains unconquerable.

उत्खातान् प्रतिरोपयन् कुसुमितांश्चिन्वन् लघून् वर्धयन्
अत्युच्चान् नमयन् पृथून् विदलयन् विश्लेषयन् संहतान्।
तीक्ष्णान् कण्टकिनो बहिर्निभमयन् स्वारोपितान् पालयन्
मालाकार इव प्रयोगकुशलो राज्ये चिरं तिष्टति॥15॥

The ruler stays long in power who acts like a skilled gardener: rehabilitating uprooted ones, watching the blooming ones, strengthening the weak, bending down the too tall ones, weakening the excessively strong ones, separating the clustered ones, trimming the thorny ones and protecting the ones that have come up by themselves.

पार्थिवस्य च भृत्यस्य वदायि गुणलक्षणम्
येन संवर्धते राजा भाण्डागारस्तथैव च॥17॥

The good quality of a ruler and a servant is that which fills the treasury and the storeroom (respectively).

परेण चिन्तितो मन्त्रो दैवेन च निवारितः।
साधुपथस्थितो राजा भगवान् दैवकिर्यथा॥16॥

A ruler who follows the right path would be like Lord Krishna, evil designs of enemies would be warded off by God's divine acts.

अनायव्ययकर्ता च अनाथः कलहप्रियः
आतुरः सर्वभक्षी च नरः शीघ्रं विनश्यति॥18॥

The spendthrift, the orphan, the quarrelsome, the sick, the one who eats everything indiscriminately perish fast.

वरं न राज्यं न कुराजराज्यं
वरं न मित्रं न कुमित्रमित्रम्।
वरं न शिष्यो न कुशिष्यशिष्यो
वरं न दारा न कुदारदाराः॥19॥

It is better not to have a ruler rather than have a

bad ruler. It is better not to have a friend rather than have a bad friend. It is better not to have a disciple rather than have a bad disciple. It is better not to have a wife rather than have a bad wife.

भोगिनः कञ्चुकासक्ताः क्रूराः कुटिलगामिनः।
फणिनो मन्त्रसाध्याश्च राजानो भुजगा इव॥21॥

Rulers are like snakes: both are hooded, fond of enjoyment and protective covering, cruel and crooked in movement, but are controllable by counsel (as snakes are controlled by mantras).

कुराजराज्येन कुतः प्रजासुखं
कुमित्रमित्रेण कुतोऽस्ति निर्वृतिः।
कुदारदारैश्च कुतो गृहे रतिः
कुशिष्यमध्यापयतः कुतो यशः॥20॥

Where is happiness for the people in a state ruled by a bad ruler? Where is happiness from a bad friend? Where is pleasure in a home from a bad wife? Where is fame to one who teaches a bad disciple?

कुमित्रे नास्ति विश्वासः कुभार्यायां कुतो रतिः
कुराज्ये नास्ति निर्वृतिः कुदेशे नास्ति जीवितम्॥22॥

There is no trust in a bad friend, no pleasure in a bad wife, no happiness under a bad ruler, no life in a bad country.

धर्मस्य मूलं राजानस्तपोमूलं च ब्राह्मणाः।
ब्राह्मणा यत्र पूज्यन्ते तत्र धर्मः सनातनः॥23॥

Rulers are the root of righteousness, Brahmins are the root of penance. Where the learned ones are worshipped, righteousness remains permanent.

आत्मवर्गं परित्यज्य परवर्गं समाश्रयेत्।
स्व्यमेव लयं याति यथा राजान्यधर्मत:॥24॥

A ruler who gives up his people and seeks others or another religion perishes.

राष्ट्रं पालयते नित्यं सत्यधर्मं परायण:।
निर्जित्य परसैन्यानि पतिधर्मेण पालयेत्॥26॥

The ruler shall rule his country, ever devoted to truth and righteousness, and defeating enemy forces protect his territory like a husband.

राज्यं च सम्पदो भोगा: कुले जन्म पवित्रता।
पाण्डित्य मायुरारोग्यं धर्म स्यैतत् फलं विदु:॥25॥

A territory to rule, riches, pleasures, noble birth, purity, scholarship, long life, health – these are all the fruits of righteousness.

कारणेन विना भृत्ये यस्तु कुप्यति पार्थिव:।
स गृह्लात विषोन्मादं कृष्णसर्पप्रदंशित:॥27॥

The ruler who without reason gets angry with his servant attracts the poison (of retaliation), as if bitten by a black cobra.

किं चित्रं यदि शब्दशास्त्रकुशलो विप्रो भवेत् पण्डित:
किं चित्रं यदि दण्डनीतिनिपुणो राजा भवेत् धार्मिक:
तच्चित्रं यदि रूपयौवनवती साध्वो भवेदङ्गना
तच्चित्रं यदि निर्धनीर्तािप पुरुष: पापं न
कुर्यात्क्ष्वचित्॥28॥

What is surprising if a Brahmin, versed in Vedic lore becomes a scholar? What is surprising if a ruler, versed in political science becomes just? That is surprising if a beautiful young lady becomes a virtuous woman. That is surprising if a poor man does not commit any sin any time.

दृढ़ा सद्भिः सभाकीर्णा दृढ़ो राजा सुधार्मिकः।
दृढ़ा पतिव्रता नारी स्थलं तृणमयं दृढ़म्॥29॥

An assembly, full of good people, is strong, a righteous ruler is strong, a virtuous woman is firm, a place full of grass is firm.

समुद्रावरणा भूमिः प्राकारावरणं गृहम्।
नरेन्द्रावरणो देशश्चारित्रावरणाः स्त्रियः॥30॥

The earth is clothed by the ocean, the house by the courtyard, the state by the ruler and women by character.

पत्यौ भक्तिर्व्रतं स्त्रीणामद्रोहो मन्त्रिणां व्रतम्।
प्रजानां पालनं राज्ञां व्रतं शीलं महात्मनाम्॥31॥

Devotion to husband is woman's duty, loyalty by ministers, protection of people is the ruler's duty, good behaviour of great souls.

अहेतुर्भ्रकुटिं नव क्षदा कुर्वीत पार्थिवः।
विना दोषेण यो भृत्यान् राजा धर्मेण पालयेत्॥32॥

Without reason and without fault, the ruler should not frown on or wound servants, he should protect them justly.

दुर्बलानामनाथानां बालवृद्धतपस्विनाम्।
अन्याय परिभूतानां सर्वेषां पार्थिवो गतिः॥35॥

The ruler is the refuge for all: the weak, the orphaned, the young, the old, the ascetics and those who have been wronged or humiliated.

दुर्बलस्य बलं राजा वालानां रोदनं बलम्।
बलं मूर्खस्य मौनित्वं चोराणामनृतं बलम्॥36॥

The ruler is strength of the weak, as crying is that of children, silence of fools, and falsehood of thieves.

शुचि भूमिगतं तोयं शुचिर्नाशे पतिव्रता।
शुचिः क्षेमकरो राजा सन्तोषी ब्राह्मणः शुचिः॥33॥

Water whcih has gone into the earth is pure, pure too are: a chaste woman, a ruler who creates welfare and a Brahmin who is satisfied.

अनाथानां दरिद्राणां बालवृद्धतपस्विनाम्।
अन्याय परिभूतानां सर्वेषां पार्थिवो गतिः॥34॥

The ruler is the refuge for all: the orphaned, the poor, the infant, the old, the recluse, the wronged and the humiliated.

राजपत्नी गुरोः पत्नी मित्रपत्नी तथैव च।
पत्नीमाता स्वमाता च पञ्चैता मातरः स्मृताः॥37॥

Five are deemed as mother: the ruler's wife, teacher's wife, friend's wife, wife's mother and one's own mother.

निर्धनं पुरुषं वेश्या प्रजा भग्नं नृपं त्यजेत्।
खगा वीतफलं वृक्षं भुक्त्वा चाभ्यागता गृहम्॥38॥

The courtesan deserts the impoverished man, people desert a weakened ruler, birds a fruitless tree, the guest deserts a house after enjoying food.

राजा धर्मेण कुर्वीत धनसंचयमेकतः।
अन्यतस्तेन सततं वर्धयेदुत्तमान् द्विजान्॥39॥

The ruler should collect riches through just means and encourage noble intellectuals.

असमर्थाः प्रकुर्वन्ति मुनयोऽप्यर्थ संचयम्।
किं न कुर्वन्ति भूपाला येषां कोशवशाः प्रजाः॥40॥

Even inept ascetics store up riches, why should not rulers, whose people are dependent on the treasury?

पुष्पं पुष्पं विचिन्वीत मूलच्छेदं न कारयेत्।
मालाकार इवारामे न यथाङ्गारकारकः॥61॥

As the gardener plucks each flower in the garden, without destroying the roots, so should the ruler collect revenue without destroying the sources.

दुग्ध्वा हि भुज्यते क्षीरं गां विक्रीय न भुज्यते।
तद्वद् दुग्धप्रयोगेण भोग्यं राष्ट्रं महीभुजा॥62॥

By proper milking is milk obtained, not by selling the cow. Similarly by due milking practice should the country be enjoyed by the ruler.

सन्धौ विरोधे दाने च यशः स्वात्मसुखोदये।
अपि मोक्षपरिप्राप्तावर्थो बन्धुर्महीभुजः॥44॥

Wealth is the friend of the ruler in the forging of treaties, in war, in making donations, winning fame, in creating happiness for oneself and attaining liberation.

यथा क्रमेण गृह्लाति पुष्पेश्यो मधु षट्पदः।
तथा वित्तमुपादाय राजा कुर्वीत संचयम्॥64॥

As the bee collects honey gradually from the flowers, so should the ruler fill up the treasury, collecting revenue gradually.

मधुक्त् कथितं राष्ट्रं न हन्तव्याश्च मधुपाः।
वत्सापेक्षी दुहेच्चैव राजा भूमिं च पालयेत्॥65॥

The state has been likened to honey, but the bees are not to be killed. The ruler should protect the land and extract revenue as well.

वल्मीकं मधुजालं च शुक्लपक्षे च चन्द्रमाः।
राजद्रव्यं च भैक्षं च स्तोकं स्तोकेन वर्धते॥66॥

The ruler's riches grow little by little, like the anthill, honeycomb and the moon in the bright fortnight.

मक्षिका व्रणमिच्छन्ति धनमिच्छन्ति पार्थिवाः।
नीचाः कलहमिच्छन्ति शान्तिमिच्छन्ति साधवः॥67॥

Rulers seek riches, as fleas seek festering wounds, low ones seek quarrels and good men seek peace.

तृप्येन्न राजा धनसंचयेन न सागरो भूरिजलागमेन
न पण्डितः साधुसुभाषितेन तृप्येन्न चक्षुः प्रियदर्शनेन॥68॥

The ruler is never satisfied with revenue collection, as the ocean with incoming waters, the scholar with good sayings and the eye with the sight of the beloved.

ब्रह्मस्वेन च पुष्टाङ्गा हस्त्यश्वरथापत्तयः।
संग्रामकाले सीदन्ति राज्ञो ब्रह्मस्वभक्षणात्॥69॥

The ruler's forces: elephants, horses and chariots are reinforced by what belongs to the Brahmins. In wartime, rulers become weak if what belongs to the Brahmins is taken away.

माता यदि विषं दद्यात् पित्रा विक्रीयते सुतः।
राजा हरति सर्वस्वं को मे त्राता भविष्यति॥233॥

If mother gives poison, the father sells son, and the ruler takes away everything, who will protect me?

काके शौचं द्यूतकारेषु सत्यं सर्पे क्षान्ति स्त्रोषु
कामोपशान्तिः।
क्लीबे धैर्यं मद्यपे तत्त्वचिन्ता राजा मित्रं केन दृष्टं श्रुतं
वा॥255॥

Who has seen or heard of a ruler as a friend, cleanliness in crows, truth in gamblers, forgiveness in serpents, satisfaction of love in women, valour in cowards, and discerning power in drunkards?

न राज्ञा सह मित्रत्वं न सर्पो निर्विषः क्वचित्।
न कुलं निर्मलं तत्र स्त्रीजनो यत्र जायते॥256॥

There can be no friendship with a ruler. There is never a non-poisonous snake. No family remains pure where a girl is born.

का प्रीतिः सह मार्जारैः का प्रीतिखनीपतौ
गणिकाभिश्च का प्रीतिः का प्रीतिर्भिक्षुकैः सह॥257॥

Where is satisfaction in cats, kings, courtesans and beggars?

विनयं राजपुत्रेभ्यः पण्डितेभ्यः सुभाषितम्।
अनृतं द्यूतकारेभ्यः स्त्रीभ्यः शिक्षेत कैतवम्॥252॥

Humility should be learnt from noble princes, good speech from scholars, falsehood from gamblers and cunning from women.

राजा वेश्या यमो ह्यग्निस्तस्करो बालयाचकौ।
परदुःखं न जानन्ति ह्यष्टमों ग्रामकूटकः॥253॥

Eight persons do not know others' sorrow: the ruler, the prostitute, death, fire, thief, infant, beggar, and the village rogue.

कोऽर्यान् प्राप्य न गर्वितो विषयिणः कस्यापदोऽस्तं गताः
स्त्रीभिः कस्य न खण्डित भुवि मनः को नाम राज्ञां प्रियः।
कः कालस्य न गोचरत्वमगमत् कोऽर्थी गतो गौरवं
को वा दुर्जनवागुराहसु पतितः क्षेमेण यातः पथि॥254॥

Who did not become arrogant on attaining riches? Which sensualist had an end of his troubles? Whose heart has not been hurt by women? Who has been (permanently) dear to rulers? Who has escaped the stealthy march of time? Which beggar had dignity? Who, fallen in bad company, has travelled safe on his path?

सुहृदामुपकारकारणाद् द्विषंतामप्यपकारकारणात्।
नृपसंश्रय इष्यते बुधैर्जठरं को न बिमर्ति केवलम्।।266।।

Wise men seek the service of rulers to help friends and destroy enemies. Who stimulates the stomach for nothing?

गुरुश्छाया पिताछाया छाया ज्येष्ठश्च बान्ध्वाः।
छाया राजसु समानमेताश्छायाः सुदुर्लभाः।।267।।

Favour of rulers is a shadow, as a good teacher, father, elder brother, relatives. These shadows are rare.

रिक्तपाणिनं पश्येत राजानं देवतां गुरुम्।
नैमित्तिकं च वैद्यं च फलेन फलमादिशेत्।।268।।

One should not see empty-handed the ruler, deity, teacher, astrologer or the doctor. With offerings results are achieved.

नास्ति मैत्रं नरेन्द्रैश्च नास्ति मैत्रं खलैः सह।
नास्ति मैत्रमबोधैश्च न च क्रीडा भुजंगमैः।।258।।

There can be no friendship with rulers, rascals, fools, as there can be no play with snakes.

स्त्रीषु राजसु सर्पेषु स्वाध्याये शत्रु विग्रहे।
अग्नौ दुर्जने विश्वास कः प्राज्ञः कर्तुमहंति।।259।।

Which wise man can place trust in rulers, women, serpents, one's own learning, in war with enemies, fire and evil men?

नखिनां च नदीनां च शृङ्गिणां शस्त्रपाणिनाम्।
विश्वासो नैव कर्त्तव्यः स्त्रीषु राजकुलेषु च।।260।।

Ruling families should not be trusted, nor women, animals with claws, rivers, creatures with horns and those who carry weapons.

गन्धः सुवर्णे फलमिक्षदण्डे नाकारि पुष्पं खलु चन्दनस्य।
विद्वान् धनाढयो नृपतिश्चिराधुर्धातुः पुरा कोऽपि
नबुद्धिदोऽभूत्॥246॥

None is wiser than the creator: gold has not been given fragrance, sugarcane has not been given fruit, sandalwood has no flower, nor is a scholar rich or a ruler long-lived.

रंक करोति राजानं राजानं रंकमेव च।
धनिनं निर्धनं चैव निर्धनं धनिनं विधिः॥247॥

God makes the ruler a beggar and a beggar a ruler, the poor rich and the rich poor.

अहिं नृपं च शार्दूलं किटिं च बालंक तथा।
परश्वानं च मूर्खं च सप्त सुप्तान् न बोधयेत्॥248॥

Seven sleeping ones should not be woken up: the ruler, the lion, the snake, the hog, the infant, another's dog, and an idiot.

अवंशपतितो राजा मूर्खपुत्रश्च पण्डितः।
अधनेन धनं प्राप्य तृणवन्मन्यते जगत्॥243॥

A ruler descended from a low family, a scholar with an idiotic son and a poor man suddenly become rich are all treated lightly by the world.

शास्त्रार्थचक्षुषा विद्वान् नरेन्द्रा नीतिचक्षुषा।
वेदार्थचक्षुषा विप्रा इतरे चर्मचक्षुषा॥244॥

Rulers should see through the eyes of justice, scholars through the eyes of learning, Brahmins through the eyes of scriptures and the rest through the surface eyes.

गन्धेन गावः पश्यन्ति वेदैः पश्यन्ति ब्राह्मणाः।
चारेः पश्यन्ति राजानश्चक्षुर्भ्यामितरे जनाः॥245॥

Rulers see through spies, as cows through smell, Brahmins through scriptures and the rest of the people through their normal eyes.

एतदर्थं हि सौमित्रे राज्यमिच्छन्ति भूभृतः।
यदेषां सर्वकार्येषु बचो न प्रतिहन्यते॥240॥

For this reason rulers desire domains: that in all matters their commands are not violated.

यच्छक्तावप्युपेक्षन्ते कदाचित् तत्र कारणम्।
समूलकाषं कषितुमुपायोऽसौ न मूढता॥241॥

Sometimes, though competent to rule, they give up (the domain) not out of foolishness, but as a touchstone to verify the truth (whether out of power their writ will run or not).

आज्ञामात्रफलं राज्यं ब्रह्मचर्यफलं तपः।
ज्ञानमात्रफला विद्या दत्तभुक्तफलं धनम्॥242॥

The fruit of the domain is command, as the fruit of penance is celibacy, the fruit of learning knowledge and of wealth donation and enjoyment.

सिंहरूपेण राजानो व्याघ्ररूपेण मन्त्रिणः।
भृत्यश्च गृध्ररूपेण क्षयं यास्यन्ति वै प्रजाः॥237॥

If the ruler is like a lion, ministers like tigers and officials are like vultures, the people are destroyed.

नक्षत्रभूषणं चन्द्रो नारीणां भूषणं पतिः।
पृथिवीभूषणं राजा विद्या सर्वस्य भूषणम्॥238॥

The ruler is the ornament of the earth, as the moon is of stars, husband of women, and learning of all.

बालोऽपि नावमन्तव्यो मनुष्य इति भूमिपः।
महती देवता ह्येषा नररूपेण तिष्ठति॥239॥

The ruler should not be despised even if he is an infant, as if he is an ordinary man. A great god exists in human form as the ruler.

यत्र राजा स्वयं चौरः समन्त्री सपुरोहितः।
तत्राहं किं करिष्यामि यतो रक्षा ततो भयम्॥234॥

Where the ruler, along with the minister and the priest, is himself a thief, what shall I do? Where there is protection there is also fear.

राज्ञि धर्मिणि धर्मिष्ठाः पापे पापाः समे समाः।
राजानमनुवर्तन्ते यथा राजा तथा प्रजाः॥235॥

If the ruler is righteous, people are righteous, if he is a sinner, the people are also sinners, if he is equal in virtue and vice, so are the people. People follow the ruler. Like ruler like people.

राजा राष्ट्रकृतं पापं राज्ञः पापं पुरोहितः।
भर्ता च स्त्रीकृतं पापं शिष्यपापं गुरुस्तथा॥236॥

The ruler is responsible for the people's sin, the priest for the ruler's sin, husband for the wife's sin and the teacher for the student's sin.

लोको यथा किल तथा न भूपतिः स्यात्
सद्भूपतिः खलु यथैव तथैव लोकाः।
धर्मप्रवृत्तिरथ तद्विपरीतवृत्तिः
कृत्स्ने जने नरपतिः प्रभवत्यशेषम्॥232॥

The ruler should not be like subjects. The people should however be like a good ruler. The ruler powerfully influences the entire people, towards righteous action or the opposite.

आज्ञाभङ्गो नरेन्द्राणां मानखण्डना।
पृथक् शय्या च नारीणामशस्त्रविहितो वधः॥230॥

Violation of the ruler's order or showing disrespect to him is like killing him without weapons. Instant sleep is likewise murdering a woman.

व्रजेद् धनार्थी वाणिज्यं विद्यार्थी च बहुश्रुतम्।
ऋतुकालमपत्यार्थी मानार्थी नृपत्रि व्रजेत्॥160॥

One who seeks fame should serve the ruler, while one who seeks wealth should take to business, one who seeks learning a reputed scholar, and one who seeks progeny should wait for the monthly period (of his wife).

समाने शोभते प्रीती राज्ञि सेवा च शोभते।
वाणिज्यं व्यवहारेषु स्त्री दिव्या शोभते गृहे॥161॥

Service with the ruler shines, as love shines among equals, trade among business activities, and a good woman in a home.

अप्रधानः प्रधानः स्याद् यदि सेवेत पार्थिवम्।
प्रधानोप्यप्रधानः स्याद् यदि सेवाविवर्जितः॥162॥।

An unimportant person becomes important, if he serves the ruler. A person devoid of such service becomes unimportant, even if he is an important person.

प्रियवाक्यप्रदानेन सर्वे तुष्यन्ति जन्तवः।
तस्मात् तदेव वक्तव्यं वचने किं दरिद्रता॥127॥

All beings are pleased by the gift of sweet words. Hence only sweet words should be spoken. Where is poverty in words?

सामना दानेन भेदेन क्रमेण च बलेन च।
सर्वथा तु सदा शत्रु र्घातनीयो नराधिपैः॥128॥

The enemy should be destroyed by rulers by all means at all times: whether by conciliation, concession, dissension or invasion.

उपकार गृहीतेन शत्रुणा शत्रु युद्धरेत्।
पादलग्नं करस्थेन कण्टकेनेव कण्टकम्॥129।

The enemy should be eradicated by taking the help of another enemy who is under obligation. Obstacles on the way can be tackled only by the stick in hand, the thorn can be extracted only by another thorn.

त्यजेदेकं कुलस्यार्थे ग्रामस्यार्थे कुलं त्यजेत्।
ग्रामं जनपदस्यार्थे आत्मार्थे पृथिवीं त्यजेत्॥148॥

The individual should be forsaken for the family's sake, the family for the sake of village, the village for the country and the earth for the sake of the self.

बलं विद्या च विप्राणां राज्ञा सैन्यं बलं तथा।
बलं वित्तं च वैश्यानां शूद्राणां चैकनिष्ठता॥149॥

The ruler's strength is the army, the Brahmin's strength is learning, the courtesan's wealth and the servant's unstinted devotion to duty.

बाहुवीर्यं बलं राज्ञो ब्राह्मणो ब्रह्मविद् बली।
रूप यौवन माधुर्यं स्त्रीणां बलमनुत्तमम्॥150॥

The ruler's strength is the valour of the army, Brahmin's knowledge of God, and women's supreme strength is the sweetness of youth and beauty.

2. Criteria to be enforced in appointments of officials

दम्भाश्रितान् कपटिनो हिंस्रानुत्साहवर्जितात्।
अशक्तान् भयभीतांश्च राजा भृत्यान् विवर्जयेत्॥204॥

The ruler should avoid appointing persons who are fraudulent, dishonest, cruel, without enthusiasm, incompetent and cowardly.

क्षान्ति भक्तिविहीनश्च विपक्षौ धनलोलुपः।
अशक्तो भयभीतश्च राज्ञा त्यक्तव्य एव सः॥205॥

Persons who have no patience or loyalty, who are inimical, miserly, incompetent and cowardly should be avoided by the ruler.

क्रूरं व्यसनिनं लुब्धमप्रगल्भं सदार्जवम्।
अनार्यं व्ययकर्तारं नाधिपत्ये नियोजयेत्॥206॥

One who is cruel, addicted to vices, miserly, timid, too outspoken, independent and spendthrift should not be appointed to positions of power.

प्राज्ञे नियोज्यमाने तु सन्ति राज्ञस्त्रयो गुणाः।
यशः स्वर्गनिवासश्च विपुलश्च धनागमः॥201॥

By deploying a wise man for a task, three benefits accrue to the ruler: fame, substantial riches and heaven.

मूर्खे नियोज्यमाने तु त्रयो दोषाः महीपतेः।
अयशश्चार्थनाशश्च नरके गमनं तथा॥202॥

If a fool is employed, three bad results afflict the ruler: ill repute, loss of wealth and descent to hell.

तस्माद् भूमीश्वरी नित्यं धर्मकामार्थवृद्ये।
गुणवन्तं नियुञ्जीत गुणहीनं विवर्जयेत्॥203॥

Hence the ruler should always appoint a person of

good qualities and avoid one without qualities so that righteousness, happiness and prosperity increase.

कण्टकस्य विमग्नस्य दन्तस्य चलितस्य च।
अमात्यस्य च दुष्टस्य मूलादुदूरणं सुखम्॥210॥

It is better that a bad minister is removed lock, stock and barrel, as an embedded thorn or a shaking tooth is to be extracted from the root.

अलसं मुखरं स्तब्ध क्रूरं व्यसनिनं शंठम्।
असन्तुष्टमभक्तं च त्यजेत् भृत्यं नराधिपः॥211॥

The ruler should give up a servant who is lazy, talkative, stupid, cruel, addicted to vices, obstinate, dissatisfied, and disloyal.

3. Superintendent of Justice

कुलशीलगुणोपेतः सर्वधर्म परायणः।
प्रवीणः प्रेषणाध्यक्षी धर्माध्यक्षी विधीयते॥212॥

The superintendent of justice should be of good family, conduct and qualities, well-versed in all laws, competent and skilled in investigation.

आत्मद्वेषाद् भवेन्मृत्यु परद्वेषाद् धनक्षयः।
राजद्वेषाद् भवेन्नाशो ब्रह्मद्वेषात् कुलक्षयः॥250॥

Hatred towards the ruler results in ruin, as hatred towards oneself results in death, hatred towards others results in decay of wealth and hatred towards the learned results in decline of the family.

4. Custodian of Inner Apartments

खञ्जः कुब्जो मन्दबुद्धिर्वृऽशक्तो जितेन्द्रियः।
निस्पृहश्च प्रयोक्तव्यो राज्ञोऽन्तः पुररक्षकः॥226॥

The custodian of the ruler's inner apartments

should be lame, hunch-backed, dull-witted, old, impotent, of controlled senses, free from desires and useful.

तुल्यार्थं तुल्यसामर्थ्यं मन्त्रज्ञं व्यवसायिनम्।
अर्धराज्यहरं भृत्यं यो न हन्यात् स हन्यते।।।209।।

The ruler who does not destroy a servant who is equal in wealth, skill, counsel, industry and who has stolen half the state is destroyed.

5. Superintendent of Horses

समस्तहयशास्त्रज्ञो वाहनेषु जितश्रमः।
शौर्यवोर्यगुणोपेतः अश्वाध्यक्षो विधीयतेः।।216।।

The superintendent of horses should know all the sciences regarding horses, unrivalled in driving (horse-drawn) vehicles, and have the qualities of bravery and valour.

6. Royal Doorkeeper

इङ्गिताकारतत्त्वज्ञो वलवान प्रियदर्शनः।
अप्रमादी सदा दक्षः प्रतीहारः स उच्यते।।217।।

The ruler's doorkeeper should be able to catch hints, strong, pleasant to look at, not careless and competent.

7. Royal Minister

अदीर्घमृत्रः स्मृतिमान् कृतज्ञो नीतिशास्त्रवित्।
धीमानायतिदर्शी च मन्त्री राज्ञः सुसन्निधिः।।218।।

The ruler's minister should be prompt in action, have a good memory, be grateful, be well-versed in political science, intelligent and far-sighted.

8. Treasury Officer

मूलवृत्तिहितो धीरः सर्वरत्नपरीक्षकः।
शुचिश्च व्यवसायी च भाण्डाध्यक्षो महीपतेः॥213॥

The ruler's official in charge of the treasury should be interested in increasing basic resources, bold, expert in the evaluation of precious stones, pure and industrious.

9. Official in Charge of Mines

प्रवीणः स्वामिनो भक्तः सत्यवादी जितेन्द्रियः।
अलुब्धः स्वधनैस्तृप्तो गञ्जाध्यक्षो महीपतेः॥214॥

The ruler's official in charge of mines should be experienced, loyal to the master, truthful, self-controlled, not greedy and satisfied with his own wealth.

10. Commander of the Army

समस्तकृतशास्त्रज्ञः पण्डितश्च जितश्रमः।
धैर्यशौर्यगुणोपेतः सेनाध्यक्षो विधीयते॥215॥

The commander of the army should know all the military sciences, be scholarly, tireless, brave and valorous.

11. Royal Secretary

सकृदुक्तगृहीतार्थो लघुहस्ती जिताक्षरः।
सर्वशास्त्रसमालोकी प्रकृष्टो नाम लेखकः॥219॥

The ruler's scribe (secretary) should understand what is spoken forthwith, write fast, have a good handwriting, well-versed in all arts and sciences and be distinguished.

मेधावी वाक्पटुः प्राज्ञः सत्यवादी जितेन्द्रियः।
सर्वशास्त्रसमालोकी एष साधुः स लेखकः॥220॥

He is the scribe, who is able, eloquent, wise, honest, who has controlled his senses, who has learnt all arts and sciences, and who is good.

12. Royal Physician

आयुर्वेदकृताभ्यासः सर्वेषां प्रियदर्शतः।
आर्यशीलगुणोपेत एष वैद्यो विधीयते॥221॥

He is the royal physician who is well-versed in Ayurveda, is pleasant-faced to everyone, and has noble conduct and qualities.

13. Royal Priest

वेदवेदाङ्गतत्त्वज्ञो जपहोमपरायणः।
आशीर्वादपरो नित्यमेष राज्ञः पुरोहितः॥222॥

He is the ruler's priest who has studied all the Vedas and Vedangas, is ever interested in offering prayers and sacrifices to God, and is always ready to bless people.

14. Royal Teacher

ज्ञानविज्ञानसम्पन्न प्रियवादी जितेन्द्रियः।
सम्यगू विद्योपदेशी च शुचिराचार्य उच्यते॥223॥

The royal teacher should be well-versed in all branches of learning, sweet-spoken, have controlled his senses, be able to impart learning well and be pure.

15. Royal Astrologer

लेखकः पाठकश्चैव गणकः प्रतिबोधकः।
ग्रहमन्त्रप्रयोक्ता च कालज्ञो राज्ञ उच्यते॥224॥

The royal astrologer should know reading, writing and arithmetic, explain well and interpret the secrets of planets.

गाम्भीर्ययुक्ता मृदुमन्दवाक्या
जितेन्द्रियाः सत्यपराः सुयोग्याः।
भाव्यर्थतज्ज्ञा विदितार्थतत्वाः
प्रायेण भृत्याः कृतिनां भवन्ति॥200॥

(The fortunate ruler's) servants are dignified, soft-spoken, self-controlled, honest, well-deployable, and have clear vision and insight.

एतदर्थं कुलीनानां नृपाः कुर्वन्ति संग्रहम्।
आदिमध्यावसानेषु न त्यजन्ति च ते नृपम्॥196॥

Rulers get hold of noble persons for this purpose: they do not desert the ruler either in the beginning, middle or the end.

दौर्मन्त्र्यान्नृपतिर्विनश्यति यतिः सङ्गात् सुतो लालनाद्
विप्रोऽनध्ययनात् कुलं कुतनयाच्छीलं खलोपासनात्।
स्त्री मद्यादनवेक्षणादपि कृषिः स्नेहः प्रवासाश्रयात्
मैत्री चाप्रणयात् समृद्धिरनयात् त्यागात् प्रमादात् ध
नम्॥183॥

The ruler perishes by bad counsel, like the recluse by attachment, son by pampering, Brahmin by non-learning, the family by bad children, conduct by evil company, woman by alcohol, agriculture by neglect, affection by absence, friendship by lack of love, abundance by indiscretion, and wealth by either sacrifice or arrogance.

कुस्त्री हन्ति कुटुम्बानि कुपुत्रो हन्ति वैकुलम्।
कुमन्त्री हन्ति राजानं राष्ट्रं चौरेण हन्यते॥184॥

The bad minister destroys the ruler, as robbers ruin the country, the bad woman families, the bad son the family.

वैद्य पानरतं नटं कुपठित स्वाध्यायहीनं द्विजं
शूरं कापुरुषं विभुं च विरसं भूर्खं परिव्राजकम्।
राजानं च कुमन्त्रिभिः परिवृतं देशं च सोपद्रवं
भार्यां यौवनगर्वितां पर रतां मुञ्चन्ति शीघ्रं बुधाः॥185॥

Wise men desert fast the ruler surrounded by evil ministers, as also the drunkard doctor, the unlettered actor, the Brahmin who has not practised his learning, a cowardly warrior, unfriendly master, foolish servant, a troubled country, a wife proud of her youth and involved in other men.

नदीतीरेषु ये वृक्षा या च नारी निराश्रया।
सामन्तरहितो राजा न भवन्ति चिरायुषः॥180॥

Rulers without ministers are not long-lived, like trees on river-banks and unsupported women.

यत् किंचित् कुरुते भृत्यः शुभं वा यदि वाशुभम्।
सुकृतं वर्धते तेन राज्ञो दुष्कृतमेव च॥181॥

Whatever the servant does, good or bad, results in good or bad for the ruler.

यत् किंचित् कुरुते भृत्यः शुभं वा यदि वाशुभम्।
तेन संवर्धते राजा सुकृतैर्दुष्कृतैरपि॥182॥

Whatever the servant does, good or bad, thereby the ruler benefits or comes to grief.

जीर्णमन्नं प्रशंसन्ति भार्यां गतयौवनाम्।
रणात् प्रत्यागतं शूरं शस्यं च गृहमागतम्॥157॥

The warrior who returns from the battlc is praised,

like the grain brought home, well-digested food and a wife whose youth is gone.

शीतभीताश्च ये विप्रा रणभीताश्च क्षत्रियाः।
अग्निभीताश्च या नारी त्रयः स्वर्गं न यान्ति हि॥158॥

Warriors who are afraid of battle do not go to heaven, as also Brahmins who are afraid of the cold and women who are afraid of the fire.

विप्रयोविप्रवह्नयोश्च दंपत्योः स्वामिभृत्ययोः।
अन्तरेण न गन्तव्यं हरस्य वृषमस्य च॥159॥

One should not go between (interfere with) two Brahmins, between the Brahmin and his fire, couples, master and servant, the bullock and the plough.

नदीतीरे च ये वृक्षाः परगेहेष कामिनी।
मन्त्रिहीनाश्च राजानः शीघ्रं नश्चन्यसंशयम्॥177॥

Rulers without ministers undoubtedly perish fast, like trees on river-banks, and beloved in others' houses.

नदीतीरेषु ये वृक्षा या च नारी निरंकुशा।
मन्त्रिहीनो भवेद् राजा तस्य राज्यं विनश्यति॥178॥

The state of a ruler without ministers perishes, like trees on river-banks and an uncontrolled woman.

नदीतीरे च ये वृक्षा। या च नारी निराश्रया।
मन्त्रिणा रहितो राजा अचिरं तस्य जीवनम्॥179॥

Short is the life of a ruler without ministers, like that of trees on river-banks and a woman without a support.

धीराणां भूषणं विद्या मन्त्रिणो राजभूषणम्।
भूषणं च पतिः स्त्रीणां शीलं सर्वस्य भूषणम्॥175॥

Ministers are the ornament of the ruler, as learning

is of brave men, husband of women, and character of everyone's.

असहायस्य कार्याणि सिद्धिं नायान्ति कानिचित्।
तस्मात् समस्त कार्येषु सहायो भूपतेर्गतिः॥176॥

A ruler has to seek assistance in all matters, since a man without assistance does not succeed in anything.

वृक्षं क्षीणफलं त्यजन्ति विहगाः शुष्कं सरः सारसाः
निर्द्रव्यं पुरुषं त्यजन्ति ललना भ्रष्टं नृपं मन्त्रिणः।
पुष्पं पर्युषितं त्यजन्ति मधुपा दग्धं वनान्तं मृगाः
सर्वः कार्यवशाज्जनोऽभिरमते कः कस्य को
वल्लभः॥174॥

The birds abandon the tree when there are no fruits, swans abandon the dried up lake, women abandon men who are no longer rich, ministers abandon a fallen ruler, bees abandon the stale flower, animals the burnt up forest. People try to please for some selfish objective. Who rules over whom?

लता पार्श्वे स्थितं वृक्षं भृत्याः पार्श्वे स्थितं नृपम्।
पार्श्वस्थं पुरुषं योषिद् वेष्टयन्ति न संशयः॥170॥

Servants encompass the ruler at their side, like the creeper, the neighbouring tree, and a woman a man constantly at her side. No doubt about this.

मन्त्रिवर्गस्य सारोऽयं दृशि निन्यं प्रसन्नता।
मुखे वहति माधुर्य हृदये कार्यनिश्चयम्॥166॥

The cardinal principle of the ruler's ministers is: cheerfulness at all times, sweetness of speech and firmness of decision at heart.

परकार्येषु युक्तात्मा स्वकार्ये क्षिप्रसाधनम्।
सुहृत्कार्येषु निर्वृत्ती राजकार्येषु विक्रमः॥167॥

(The minister should be able to) suggest strategy in

enemy's affairs, take quick action in own affairs, exhibit happiness in friend's achievements and boldness in state affairs.

परीक्ष्य प्रथमं भृत्यानुत्तमाधममध्यमान्।
योजयेत् तादृशेष्वेव नृपतिः स्वेषु कर्मसु॥190॥

The ruler should deploy servants for the various tasks after finding out whether they are of superior quality, low or mediocre.

अनभ्यासैर्हता विद्या नित्यहासैर्हताः स्त्रियः।
कुबीजेन हतं क्षेत्रं भृत्यदोषैर्हता नृपाः॥186॥

Rulers are ruined by the faults of their servants, as learning is by non-practice, women by daily merriment, and the field by bad seed.

देवो राजा गुरुर्भार्या वैद्यनक्षत्रपाठकाः।
रिक्तहस्ता न गच्छन्ति गते कार्यं न सिध्यति॥269॥

Deity, ruler, teacher, wife, doctor, astrologer, if visited empty-handed, do not bestow desired objects.

भेतव्यमकुलीनानां राज परोपजीविनाम्।
भेतव्यं ज्ञातशत्रूणां ज्ञात्वा पूर्वापकारिणम्॥261॥

Ignoble ones should be feared, as rulers should be feared. As also those who depend on others for a living. Known enemies should also be feared, knowing their previous misdeed.

उन्मत्तानां भुजङ्गानां मद्यपानां च दन्तिनाम्।
स्त्रीणां राजकुलानां च विश्वसन्ति गतायुषः॥262॥

Only those whose life-span is over will trust mad people, snakes, drunkards, elephants, women and ruling families.

शास्त्रं सुचिन्तितमपि प्रतिचिन्तनीयम्
आराधितोऽपि नृपतिः परिशंकनीयः।
अंके स्थितापि युवतिः परिरक्षणीया
शास्त्रे नृपे च युवतौव शतावसन्नाः॥263॥

Learning, considered to be well learnt, should again be mastered, the ruler, though well disposed, should be suspected, young woman, though situated on one's body, should be guarded. Attachment of learning, rulers and young women is fleeting.

अग्निरापः स्त्रियो मूर्खाः सर्पा राजकूलानि च।
नित्यं यत्नेन सेव्यानि सद्यः प्राणहराणि षट्॥264॥

Six things should be dealt with care, they destroy life instantaneously: ruling families, fire, water, women, serpents, and idiots.

अत्यासन्ना विनशाय दूरस्था न फलप्रदाः।
सेव्यतां मध्यभगेन राजा वाह्नर्गुरूः स्त्रियः॥265॥

Very close proximity means disaster, being at a distance is non-productive of results. A middle path is right with rulers, fire, teacher and women.

असंतुष्टा द्विजा नष्टाः संतुष्टाश्च महीभृतः
सलज्जा गणिका नष्टा निर्लज्जाश्च कुलाङ्गनाः॥92॥

Rulers who are satisfied are lost, dissatisfied Brahmins are lost, modest courtesans are lost as also immodest family women.

अग्निर्दहति तापेन सूर्यो दहति रश्मिभिः।
राजा दहति दण्डेन तपसा ब्राह्मणो दहेत्॥93॥

The ruler burns by punishment, fire by heat, sun by its rays, and the Brahmin by his penance.

सर्वो दण्डजितो लोको दुर्लभो हि शुचिर्नरः।
दण्डस्य हि भयात् सर्वं जगद् भोगाय कल्पते॥94॥

People are controlled by punishment, the intrinsically pure man is rare. Out of fear of punishment the world enjoys blessings.

अक्षेषु मृगयायां च स्त्रोषु पाने वृथाटने।
निद्रायां च निबन्धेन क्षिप्रं नश्यति भूपतिः॥89॥

The ruler addicted to dice, hunting, women, drinking, aimless wandering and sleep perishes fast.

लंघयेच्छात्रमर्यादां हेतुवादेन यो नरः
स नश्यति पुनः क्षिप्रमिह लोके परत्रः च॥90॥

He who violates established righteous practices by logic or argument perishes fast in this world and the hereafter.

लीलां करोति यो राजा भृत्यवित्तैश्च गर्वितः।
संवादे विग्रहे क्षिप्रं रिपुभिः परिभूयते॥91॥

The ruler who indulges in pleasure-making and is proud of retinue and wealth is easily captured by enemies.

अविनीतो भृत्यजनो नृपतिरदाता शठानि मित्राणि।
अविनयवती च भार्या मस्तक शूलानि चत्वारि॥87॥

The ruler who does not donate, impertinent servants, obstinate friends and an impudent wife – these four pierce the head like spears.

लीलासुखानि भोग्यानि त्यजेदिह महीपतिः।
सुखप्रवृत्ताः साध्यन्ते शात्रवैर्विग्रहे स्थितैः॥88॥

The ruler should give up pleasures and enjoyments. Those addicted to pleasures are likely to fall into the hands of enemies.

चरित्रमकृतं धर्म्यं कृतं चान्यैः प्रवर्तयेत्।
प्रवर्तयेत्नचाधर्म्यं कृतं चान्यैर्निवर्तयेत्।।26।।

(A ruler) should introduce righteous customs, practised by others but not yet current in the country. He shall not introduce unrighteous customs and should stop these if practised by others.

नास्य गुह्यं परे विद्युः छिद्रं विद्यात् परस्य च।
गूहेत् कूर्म इवाङ्गानि यत् स्याद्विवृतमात्मनः।।27।।

His (the ruler's) secret others should not get; but he should ascertain others' weak spots. As the tortoise withdraws its limbs, he should try to hide any part of his which might have been thrown open.

यथा लीनस्सर्पः यस्माद्भयं पश्चति तत्र विषमुत्सृजति।
एवमयं राजापि जातदोषाशंकः क्रोधविषमुत्सृजति।।28।।

Just as a hidden snake emits poison on whatever is seen as a threat by it, so the ruler emits the poison of anger on whomsoever from where danger is apprehended.

यथा श्वगणिनां धेनुः श्वभ्यो दुग्धे न ब्राह्मणेभ्यः।
एवमयं राजाऽपि सत्वप्रज्ञावाक्यशक्तिहीनेभ्यो दुग्ध
नात्मगुणसम्पन्नेभ्यः।।29।।

Just as the cow kept by dog-keepers gives milk to dogs and not to Brahmins, so the (depraved) ruler gives succour to those devoid of valour, wisdom, eloquence and strength and not to those of noble character.

धीराः कृच्छ्रमपि प्राप्ता न भवन्ति विषादिनः
प्रविश्य वदनं राहोः किं नोदेति पुनः शशी।।77।।

Brave men do not become sad when they beget trouble. Does not the moon which enters the dragonhead's mouth again come out?

प्राज्ञः स्निग्धो महीपालश्छिद्र कर्मबिवर्जितः।
विदूरे च परित्यागी समं दुःखं समं सुखम्॥78॥

The ruler should be wise, friendly, flawless in his dealings, keep distance, be sacrificing and equally disposed towards pain and pleasure.

गान्धर्वं नृत्तमालेख्यं वाद्यं च गणितं कलाः
अर्थशास्त्रं धनुर्वेदं यत्नाद् रक्षेन्महीपतिः॥75॥

The ruler should painstakingly protect political science, archery, art of love, dance, accountancy, music, mathematics and the fine arts.

मनस्तापं न कुर्वीत विपदं प्राप्य पार्थिवः।
आत्मनश्चोदयं शसेन्न स्याद् दुःखी न वा सुखी॥76॥

The ruler should not be disheartened when misfortune comes, he should also not feel elated in prosperity. He should be neither happy nor sad.

जात्यन्धोपि वर राजा न तु शास्त्रविवर्जितः।
अन्धः पश्यति चारेण शास्त्रहीनो न पश्यति॥73॥

A ruler born blind is better than one devoid of learning. The blind one can see through spies, but the one devoid of learning cannot.

एकं हन्यान्न वा हन्यादिषुर्मुक्तो धनुष्मता।
बुद्धिर्बुद्धिमतोन्सृष्टा हन्याद् राष्ट्रं सराजकम्॥74॥

The arrow shot by the one with the bow may or may not kill one person. But the thought of an intelligent person can destroy a country with its ruler.

सकृज्जल्पन्ति राजानः सकृज्जल्पन्ति पण्डिताः।
सकृत् कन्याः प्रदीयन्ते त्रीण्येतानि सकृत् सकृत्॥231॥

Rulers speak only once, scholars speak only once, girls are given in marriage only once. All these three happen only once.

16. Guidance for Royal Appointments: Ambassador

मेधावी वाक्पटुः प्राज्ञः परचित्तोपलक्षकः।
धीरो यथोक्तवादी च एष दूती विधीयते॥228॥

The ruler's envoy (ambassador) is one who is able, eloquent, wise, capable of knowing others' minds, brave, and speaks aptly.

प्रगल्भी बुद्धिमान् वक्ता परचित्तोपलक्षकः।
धीरो यथोक्तवादी च दूत इत्यभिधीयते॥229॥

The ruler's envoy (ambassador) is one who is competent, intelligent, eloquent, capable of knowing others' minds, brave, and speaks aptly.

मृदुनैव मृदुं हन्ति मृदुना हन्ति दारुणम्।
नासाध्यं मृदुना किंचित् तस्मात् तीक्ष्णतरो मृदुः॥131॥

(Enemies), gentle or violent, are destroyed by gentle means. Nothing is impossible by deploying gentle means. Hence gentle means are sharper (in achieving ends).

बहूनां चैव सत्त्वानां समवायो रिपुंजयः।
वर्षधाराधरो मेघस्तृणैरपि निवार्यते॥132॥

The union of a large number of good people can defeat the enemy. The cloud which rains torrentially is withstood by clusters of grass.

बहूनामप्यसाराणां समवायो हि दुःसहः।
तृणैरावेष्टयते रज्जुस्तया हस्त्यपि बध्यते॥133॥

The union of even small people can become irresistible. The elephant is tied by the rope, made of grass.

पठ पुत्र सदा नित्यमक्षरं हृदये कुरु।
स्वदेशे पूज्यते राजा विद्यां सर्वत्र पूज्यते॥71॥

Read, son, always. Memorise what you learn. The ruler is worshipped in his country. Learning is worshipped everywhere.

विद्वत्वं च नृपत्वं च नैव तुल्यं कदाचन
स्वदेशे पूज्यते राजा विद्वान् सर्वत्र पूज्यते॥72॥

Rulership and scholarship are never equal. The ruler is respected in his country, the scholar everywhere.

मनसा चिन्तितं कार्यं वचसा न प्रकाशयेत्।
मन्त्रेण रक्षयेद् गूढं कार्ये चापि नियोजयेत्॥138॥

The task conceived of in the mind should not be divulged in words. The secret, guarded through code, should be deployed in action.

17. Dealing with Enemies

गोपयेत् स्वानि रन्ध्राणि पररन्ध्राणि चिन्तयेत्।
कुसीदेन निवर्तेत राज्यमिच्छन् नृपः स्थिरम्॥139॥

One's own weaknesses should be hidden, enemy's weaknesses should be investigated. A ruler desiring a permanent kingdom should function like a moneylcndcr.

षण्मासमथवा वर्षं सन्धिं कुर्यान्नराधिपः।
आत्मनो बलमालोक्य पश्चाच्छत्रुं निपातयेत्॥140॥

The ruler should conclude a treaty of peace for six months or a year. Thercafter, keeping in view one's strength, floor the enemy.

महानदीप्रतरणं महापुरुषविग्रहम्।
महाजनविरोधं च दूरतः परिवर्जयेत्॥154॥

The crossing of a great (turbulent) river, fight with great men, enmity of a large number of people should all be avoided (by the ruler).

घासमिन्धनमन्नाद्यं शस्त्राणि विविधानि च।
दुर्गे प्रवेशनीयानि सततं शत्रुशंकया॥155॥

Fodder, fuel and food, and various weapons should always be kept in a fortress, in anticipation of enemy's attack.

उपसर्गेऽन्यचक्रे च दुर्भिक्षे च भयावहे।
असाधुजनसंपर्के चः पालयेत् स जीवतिः॥156॥

In epidemic, foreign invasion, famine and when evil men join together, he who flees lives.

हतं ज्ञानं क्रियाहीनं हताश्चाज्ञानिनः क्रियाः।
हतं निर्नायक सैन्यं स्त्रियो नष्टा ह्यभर्तृकाः॥151॥

The army without a commander is lost, as also learning without activity, actions of illiterates and women without husbands.

हतमश्रोत्रिय श्राद्धं हतो यज्ञस्त्वदक्षिणः।
हता रूपवती वन्ध्या हतं सैन्यमनायकम्॥152॥

The army without a commander is lost, like a beautiful barren woman, a sacrifice without donation and an offering to the dead without a priest.

आलस्योपहता विद्या परहस्तगताः स्त्रियः।
अल्पबीजं हतं क्षेत्रं हतं सैन्यमनायकम्॥153॥

The army without a commander is lost, like the learning of a lazy person, women who are entrusted to others, a field with inadequate seed.

अनायका विनश्यन्ति नश्यन्ति बहुनायकाः।
स्त्रीनायका विनश्यन्ति नश्यन्ति शिशुनायकाः॥104॥

Countries which have no leaders perish, as do those with many leaders, women leaders or child leaders.

अनायके न वस्तव्यं न वसेद् बहुनायके।
स्त्रीनायक न वस्तव्यं न वसेद् बालनायके॥105॥

One should not stay in a country which is leaderless, has many leaders, a woman leader or a child leader.

वसेन्मानाधिके स्थाने मानहीनं विवर्जयेत्।
मानहीनं सुरैः सार्धं विमानमपि वर्जयेत्॥109॥

One should stay where there is abundance of respect. One should avoid a place where there is no respect. One should avoid even an air chariot with angels if there is no respect.

From Chanakya Sutras

राज्यतन्त्रेप्वायत्तौ तन्त्रावापौ॥44॥

Internal administration and foreign relations are dependent on state policy.

तन्त्रं स्वविषयकृत्येष्वायत्तम्॥45॥

Deployment of the fourfold policy (conciliation, donation, division, and punishment) in one's own country is internal administration.

आवापो मण्डलनिविष्टः॥46॥

Foreign policy is deployment of the same (fourfold means) towards (neighbouring) states.

सन्धिविग्रहयोनिर्मण्डलः॥47॥

Neighbouring states are the source of treaties and

hostilities.

नीतिशास्त्रानुगो राजा॥48॥

A ruler should follow political science.

अनन्तरप्रकृतिः शत्रुः॥49॥

A ruler with contiguous territory is a rival.

एकान्तरितं मित्रमिष्यते॥50॥

The ruler next to the adjoining one is to be deemed a friend.

हेतुतः शत्रु मित्रे भविष्यतः॥51॥

Friendship and enmity result from some cause.

हीयमानः सन्धि कुर्वंति॥52॥

The one who is facing defeat should make peace.

तेजो हि सन्धानहेतुस्तदर्थानाम्॥53॥

Power is the cause of an alliance.

नातप्तलोहो लोहेन संधीयते॥54॥

Unheated metal does not coalesce with metal.

बलवान् हीनेन विगृह्लीयात्॥55॥

The strong ruler should fight the weak.

न ज्यायसा समेन वा॥56॥

One should not fight with a superior or equal.

गजपादयुद्धमिव बलवद्विग्रहः॥57॥

Fight with a stronger one is like that of the infantry with the elephant force.

आमपात्रमामेन सह विनश्यति॥58॥

An unbaked vessel on colliding with another unbaked vessel gets destroyed. (Hence equals should also not fight.)

अरिप्रयत्नमभिसमीक्षेत॥59॥

Enemy's efforts should be watched.

सन्धार्यक्तो वा॥60॥

When there are many enemies, treaty should be entered into with one.

अमित्रविरोधादात्मरक्षामावसेत्॥61॥

One's security should be guarded from the enemy's anger.

शक्तिहीनो बलवन्तमाश्रयेत्॥62॥

The weak should seek refuge in the strong.

दुर्बलाश्रयो दुःखमावहति॥63॥

Refuge in the weak results in sorrow.

अग्निवद्राजानमाश्रयेत्॥64॥

A ruler should be approached like fire.

राज्ञः प्रतिकूल नाचरेत्॥65॥

One should not act against the ruler.

उद्धतवेषधरो न भवेत्॥66॥

One should not wear provocative clothes.

न देवचरितं चरेत्॥67॥

One should not imitate the ways of gods.

द्वयोरपीर्ष्यतोर्द्वैधीभावं कुर्वीत॥68॥

When two persons quarrel, one should maintain an attitude of duplicity.

न व्यसनपरस्य कार्यावाप्तिः॥69॥

One addicted to vices does not accomplish tasks.

नासहायस्य मन्त्रनिश्चयः॥16॥

One without an adviser has no certainty of counsel.

नैकं चक्रं परिभ्रमयति॥17॥

One wheel does not move (the vehicle).

सहायः समसुखदुखः॥18॥

The true aide serves alike in prosperity and adversity.

मानी प्रतिमानिनमात्मनि द्वितीयं मन्त्रमुत्पादयेत्॥19॥

A self-respecting ruler should appoint as counsellor one who is inferior to him and respects him.

अविनीतं स्नेहमात्रेण न मन्त्रे कुर्वीत॥20॥

He should not take into counsel out of love one who is impertinent.

श्रुतवन्तमुपधाशुद्धं मन्त्रिणं कुर्वीत॥21॥

One who is learned and free from fraud should be made a minister.

मन्त्रमूलाः सर्वारम्भाः॥22॥

All things begin with counsel.

मन्त्ररक्षणे कार्यसिद्धिर्भवति॥23॥

Accomplishment of the task depends on guarding the secret of counsel.

मन्त्रविस्रावी कार्यं नाशयति॥24॥

One who lets out counsel destroys the tasks.

प्रमादाद् द्विषतां वशमुपयास्यति॥25॥

Defection to the enemy takes place due to negligence.

सर्वद्वारेभ्यो मन्त्रो रक्षितव्यः॥26॥

Ministerial advice should be kept secret from all quarters.

मन्त्रसम्पदा राज्यं वर्धते॥27॥

The country prospers by proper ministerial counsel.

श्रेष्ठतमां मन्त्रगुप्तिमाहुः॥28॥

The secrecy of ministerial counsel is of supreme importance.

कार्यान्धस्य प्रदीपो मन्त्रः॥29॥

Counsel is a beacon to the one blind of action.

मन्त्रचक्षुषा परच्छिद्राण्यवलोकयन्ति॥30॥

Through ministerial eyes others' weaknesses are seen.

मन्त्रकाले न मत्सरः कर्त्तव्यः॥31॥

At the time of taking ministerial advice there should be no quarrels.

त्रयाणामेकवाक्ये सम्प्रत्ययः॥32॥

A decision should be taken on the unanimous opinion of three (counsellors).

कार्याकार्यतत्त्वार्थदर्शिनो मन्त्रिणः॥33॥

Counsellors (ministers) are the ones who see the

true implications of what ought to be done and what ought not be done.

प्रकृतिसम्पदा ह्यनायकमपि राज्यं नीयते॥12॥

If the people are prosperous, even a leaderless state can be governed.

प्रकृतिकोपः सर्वकोपेभ्यो गरीयान्॥13॥

People's fury is the greatest of furies.

आवनीतस्वामिलाभादस्वामिलाभः श्रेयान्॥14॥

To be without a master is better than having an arrogant master.

सम्पाद्यात्मानमन्विच्छेत् सहायवान्॥15॥

After equipping oneself fully, one should seek an ally (aide).

अमित्रो दण्डनीत्यामायत्तः॥78॥

An enemy should be won over by the use of political science.

दण्डनीतिमधितिष्ठन् प्रजा संरक्षति॥79॥

Practising political science, the ruler protects the people.

दण्डः सम्पदा योजयति॥80॥

The sceptre links one to riches.

दण्डाभावे मन्त्रिवर्गाभावः॥81॥

In the absence of the sceptre, there are no ministers.

न दण्डादकार्याणि कुर्वन्ति॥82॥

Due to (fear of) the punishing rod, people do not do things which should not be done.

दण्डनीत्यामायत्तमात्मरक्षणम्॥83॥

One's self-protection is dependent on the practice of political science.

आत्मनि रक्षिते सर्वं रक्षितं भवति॥84॥

In self-protection, all are protected.

आत्मायत्तौ वृद्धिविनाशौ॥85॥

Advancement and decay are dependent on oneself.

दण्डो हि विज्ञाने प्रणीयते॥86॥

The sceptre should be wielded wisely.

2
Society and Ethics

1. Ethical Roots

सुखस्य मूलं धर्मः॥1॥
Righteousness is the root of happiness.

धर्मस्य मूलमर्थः॥2॥
Wealth is the root of righteousness.

अर्थस्य मूलं राज्यम्॥3॥
The state is the root of wealth.

राज्यमूलमिन्द्रियजयः॥4॥
Victory over senses is the root of the state.

इन्द्रियजयस्य मूलं विनयः॥5॥
Humility is the root of sense control.

विनयस्य मूलं वृद्धोपसेवा॥6॥
Worship of elders is the root of humility.

निकृतिप्रिया नीचाः॥202॥
The low-minded are fond of deception.

नीचस्य मतिर्न दातव्या॥203॥
The low-minded should not be given good advice.

तेषु विश्वासो न कर्त्तव्यः॥204॥
They (the low-minded) should never be trusted.

सुपूजितोऽपि दुर्जनः पीडयत्येव॥205॥
The evil one harms, even if treated well.

चन्दनादीनपि दावोऽग्निर्दहत्येव॥206॥

The forest fire burns even trees like sandalwood.

कदाऽपि पुरुषं नावमन्येत॥207॥

No one should ever be disrespected.

क्षन्तव्यमिति पुरुषं न बाधेत॥208॥

One who is to be pardoned should not be harassed.

भर्त्राधिक रहस्युक्तं वक्तुमिच्छन्त्यबुद्धयः॥209॥

The foolish wish to speak out what was spoken in secret by the master.

अनुरागस्तु फलेन सूच्यते॥210॥

Love is indicated by its fruit.

अतिदीर्घोऽपि कणिकारो न मुसली॥454॥

However big, the karnikara tree cannot be used to make clubs.

अतिदीप्तोऽपि खद्योतो न पावकः॥455॥

Even the brightest firefly is not fire.

न प्रवृद्धत्वं गुणहेतुः॥456॥

Mere growth cannot create quality.

सुजीर्णोऽपि पिचुमन्दो न शंक लायते॥457॥

Even if very old, a neem tree cannot be used as a shaft.

यथा बीजं तथा निष्पत्तिः॥458॥

Like the seed, the fruit.

यथा श्रुतं तथा बुद्धिः॥459॥

Intellect depends on education.

यथा कुलं तथाऽऽचारः॥460॥

Conduct depends on the family.

संस्कृतः पिचुमन्दः सहकारो न भवति॥461॥

Even with refinement, the neem does not become mango.

न चागतं सुख त्यजेत्॥462॥

A comfort which has been obtained should not be given up.

इन्द्रियवशवर्ती चतुरङ्गवानपि विनश्यति॥70॥

Even one with a fourfold army is destroyed if he is a slave of the senses.

नास्ति कार्यं द्यूतप्रवृत्तस्य॥71॥

One addicted to gambling does not accomplish anything.

मृगयापरस्य धर्मार्थौ विनश्यतः॥72॥

The ruler addicted to hunting loses his rightousness and wealth.

अर्थेषणा न व्यसनेपु गणयते॥73॥

Desire for wealth is not considered a vice.

न कामासक्तस्य कार्यानुष्ठानम्॥74॥

The lust-ridden (ruler) cannot perform his task.

अग्निदाहादपि विशिष्टं वाक्पारुष्यम्॥75॥

Sting of words is stronger than the burning of fire.

2. Advice for Rulers

दण्डपारुष्यात् सर्वजनद्वेष्यो भवति॥76॥

By excessively cruel punishment, (the ruler) becomes hated by all.

अर्थतोषिणं श्रीः परित्यजति॥77॥

Prosperity abandons one who is satisfied with wealth.

स्वयमेव दुःखमधिगच्छति॥463॥

One's actions are the cause of one's sorrow.

रात्रिचारणं न कुर्यात्॥464॥

One should not wander at night.

न चार्धरात्रं स्वपेत्॥465॥

One should not sleep for half the night only (but the whole night soundly).

तद् बिद्वद्‌िभः परीक्षेत॥466॥

Discussion about God and reality should be held with learned persons.

परगृहमकारणतो न प्रविशेत्॥467॥

One should not enter another's house without a reason.

ज्ञात्वाऽपि दोषमेव करोति लोकः॥468॥

People do wrong things knowing fully well what they are doing.

शास्त्रप्रधाना लोकवृत्तिः॥469॥

Living should be according to the scriptures.

शास्त्राभावे शिष्टाचारमनुगच्छेत्॥470॥

In the absence of a knowledge of the scriptures, the conduct of good people should be followed.

दोपवर्जितानि कार्याणि दुर्लभानि॥105॥

Flawless jobs are rare.

दुरनुबन्धं कार्यं नारभेत॥106॥

A work which is obstacle-ridden should not be started.

कालवित् कार्यं साधयेत्॥107॥

One who knows the (opportune) time accomplishes the task.

कालातिक्रमानत् काल एव फलं पिबति॥108॥

Due to lapse of time, time itself consumes the fruit.

क्षणं प्रति कालविक्षेपं न कुर्यात् सर्वकृत्येपु॥109॥

In all tasks, one should not delay even for a moment.

देशफलविभागौ ज्ञात्वा कार्यमारभेत॥110॥

One should commence a work after understanding the country and the consequences.

दैवहीनं कार्यं सुसाधमपि दुःसाधं भवति॥111॥

Without God's grace, even an easy task becomes difficult to accomplish.

नीतिज्ञो देशकालौ परीक्षेत॥112॥

The wise one should consider the (interests) of the country and the times.

परीक्ष्यकारिणि श्रीश्चिरं तिष्ठति॥113॥

Prosperity lasts long for one who acts after proper consideration.

प्रज्यक्षपरोक्षानुमानैः कार्याणि परीक्षेत॥132॥

Things should be examined with reference to facts, patent and latent, and inferences.

अपरीक्ष्यकारिणं श्रीः परित्यजति॥133॥

Prosperity forsakes one who does things without proper examination.

परीक्ष्य तार्या विपत्तिः॥134॥

Danger should be overcome after proper analysis.

स्वशक्तिं ज्ञात्वा कार्यमारभेत॥135॥

One should begin a venture after assessing one's strength.

स्वजनं तर्पयित्वा यः शेषभोजी सोऽमृतभोजी॥136॥

He feeds on nectar who first feeds his people and then eats the left-overs.

सर्वानुष्ठानादायमुखानि वर्धन्ते॥137॥

By undertaking all kinds of activities, the ways to profit develop.

नास्ति भीरोः कार्यचिन्ता॥138॥

The coward does not think of action.

स्वामिनः शीलं ज्ञात्वा कार्यार्थी कार्यं साधयेत्॥139॥

The favour-seeker accomplishes his end after knowing the nature of his master.

3. Training and Learning

क्रिया द्रव्यं हि विनयतिए नाद्रव्यम्॥169॥

Training can impart discipline to those who are suitable material, not to those who are not.

शुश्रूषाश्रवणग्रहणधारणविज्ञानोहापोहतत्त्वाभि-
निविष्टबुद्धिं विद्या विनयति नेतरम्॥170॥

Learning disciplines those whose intellects have the

desire to learn, capacity to listen attentively, power to grasp what is taught, to retain it in memory, discriminate between the important and the unimportant, draw inferences, deliberate and imbibe the truth and not others.

नवं हि द्रव्यं येन येनार्थजातेनोपदिह्यते
तत्तदाचूषति, एवमयं नवबुद्धिः यद्यदुच्येत
तत्तच्छास्त्रोपदेशमिवाभिजानाति॥171॥

A young intellect is apt to consider whatever is told as the teaching of scientific knowledge, just as a fresh, raw object absorbs whatever material it is brought in contact with.

महादोषमबुद्धबोधनम्॥172॥

Teaching wrong things is a great crime.

विद्यानां तु यथास्वमाचार्यप्रामाण्याद्विनयो नियमश्च॥173॥

Discipline and self-control are acquired by learning the various sciences under the authoritative control of concerned teachers.

ताभिर्धर्मार्थौ यद्विद्यात् तद्विद्यानां विद्यात्वम्॥174॥

That learning is called learning from which result righteousness and wealth.

विद्याबुद्धिपौरुषाभिजनकर्मातिशयतश्च पुरुषाः
पूज्याः॥175॥

Persons standing out on account of their learning, intellect, valour, noble lineage and good deeds are venerated.

एवं शास्त्रमिदं युक्तं एताभिः तन्त्रयुक्तिभिः।
अवाप्तौ पालने चोक्तं लोकस्यास्य परस्य च॥176॥

Thus this science has been propounded citing

stratagems and devices for the acquisition and protection of this world and the other.

धर्ममर्थं च कामं च प्रवर्तयति पाति च॥177॥

(This science) creates and preserves righteousness, wealth and physical pleasures.

अधर्मानर्थविद्वेषानिदं शास्त्रं निहन्ति च॥178॥

It destroys unrighteousness, poverty and hatred.

श्रुताद्धि प्रज्ञो पजायते, प्रज्ञया योगः,
योगादात्मवत्ता॥179॥

It is from learning that the intellect is formed, through the intellect skill in action (yoga) and from yoga self-control follows.

4. Philosophy

धर्माधर्मौ त्रय्यां, अर्थानर्थौ वार्तायां,
नयापनयौ दण्डनीत्यां, एतासां बलाबले
हेतुभिरन्वीक्षमाणा आन्वीक्षिकी लोकस्योपकरोति,
व्यसने अभ्युदये च बुद्धिमवस्थापयति,
प्रज्ञावाक्यक्रियावैशारद्यं च करोति॥180॥

The three Vedas deal with righteousness and unrighteousness, economics deals with wealth and poverty, politics deals with good and bad state policies. Philosophy, which sifts with reason the relative importance of these sciences, benefits the world, keeps the intellect steady in adversity and prosperity and creates excellence in thought, word and deed.

प्रदीपः सर्वविद्यानामुपायः सर्वकर्मणाम्।
आश्रयस्सर्वधर्माणां शश्वदान्वीक्षिकी मता॥181॥

Philosophy is considered the light of all learning, the means for the accomplishment of all tasks, and the refuge of all righteous beliefs (of all religions).

5. Miscellaneous Dicta

पुरुषवद्धि राज्यम्, अपुरुषा गौर्वन्ध्येव किं दुहीत?॥182॥

A state is that which has people. Without people what will it yield, like a barren cow? (Nothing).

न ह्यजनो जनपदः, अजनपदं वा राज्यं भवति॥183॥

An unpeopled territory is no country and without a country there is no state.

शक्यारम्भी विषह्यं कर्मारभेत, कल्यारम्भी
निर्दोषं, भव्यारम्भी कल्याणोदयम्॥184॥

One who embarks upon only what is possible undertakes works which are easy to accomplish, one who embarks upon only auspicious works undertakes faultless works, one who embarks upon only productive undertaking takes up works which lead to (people's) welfare.

कालश्च सकृदभ्येति नरं वै कालकांक्षिणम्।
दुर्लभस्स पुनस्तस्य कालः कर्म चिकीर्षतः॥185॥

Time (opportunity) approaches a man desirous of it only once. And will not come a second time when he wants to do his work.

प्रायशो हि कितवाः कूटवेदिनः॥186॥

Generally gamblers are crooks.

प्रणिपातेन ब्राह्मणबलं परोऽभिहारयेत्॥187॥

By prostration, an army of the learned class (Brahmins) can be won over.

सुमहताप्यर्थेन न कश्चन शरीरविनाशमिच्छेत्॥188॥

Even for the sake of immense wealth, no one desires to die.

सामान्या हि पथि सिद्धिश्चासिद्धिश्च॥189॥

Success and failure are common on all paths.

बलं हि चित्तं विकरोति॥190॥

Power alters the mind.

ताद्दशाः तादृशैरेव बोद्धव्याः॥191॥

Persons of a particular type can be found out only by those of the same type.

सुखोपरुद्धाः हि पुत्राः पितरं नाभिद्रुह्यन्ति॥192॥

Sons kept engaged in pleasures do not rise against the father.

पराक्रमो हि व्यसनमपहन्ति॥193॥

Only the display of valour can tackle trouble.

यतः श्रेयस्ततो व्रजेत्॥194॥

That course of action should be followed which will usher in prosperity.

सहस्रेषु हि मुख्यो भवत्येको न वा॥195॥

Among thousands there is hardly one or not even one (fit to be a) leader.

महत्यवकाशे हि स्थाल्याश्चानूप्याश्चौषधयो भवन्ति॥196॥

In vast tracts, medicinal herbs are found to grow in water or land very rarely.

दैवमानुषं हि कर्म लोकं यापयति॥197॥

It is the combined acts of God and man that make the world function.

अविश्वास्यो ह्यग्निः दैवपीडनं च॥198॥

Fire is not reliable and is an infliction of God.

सर्वसमयवित् आशुग्रन्थः चार्वक्षरः
लेखनवाचनसमर्थश्च हि लेखकः स्यात्॥199॥

A writer should know all conventions, he should be fast in composing, have a beautiful handwriting and be able to read documents.

कर्मारम्भाणां योगाराधनः व्यायामः॥202॥

Activity is that which brings to fruition tasks undertaken.

कर्मफलोपभोगानां क्षेमाराधनः शमः॥203॥

Peace is that which allows the enjoyment of results without disturbance.

नदीभातृकं हि स्वाजीवं, अपाश्रयश्चापदि भवति॥204॥

Land, watered by a river, is a means to living, in difficulties it becomes a support.

चित्तमनित्यं हि मनुष्याणाम्॥205॥

Men's minds are not steady.

अश्वसधर्माणो हि मनुष्याः नियुक्ताः कर्मसु
विकुर्वते॥206॥

Having a nature similar to horses, men when engaged in work, exhibit change of behaviour.

अशुचयो हि कारवः॥207॥

Artisans are generally dishonest.

विक्रमाधिकोऽपि हस्तिनमिव लुब्धकः प्राज्ञः
शूरमतिसः॥208॥

Even in matters of excessive valour, the wise one behaves like the brave one, as the hunter does the elephant.

एकं हन्यान्न वां हन्यादिषुः क्षिप्तो धनुष्मता।
प्राज्ञेन तु मतिः क्षिप्ता हन्यात् गर्भगतानपि॥209॥

The arrow shot by the archer may or may not kill a single person. But stratagem devised by a wise man can kill babes in the womb.

नित्यश्चास्य विद्यावृद्धसंयोगः विनयवृद्धयर्थम्,
तन्मूलत्वाद्विनयस्य॥210॥

In order to develop discipline, one should daily have the company of learned elders, who are firmly rooted in discipline.

सातत्येन हि निशि प्रदीपे मातरि च मृतायां
दीव्यत्येव कितवः, कृच्छ्रे च प्रतिपृष्टः कुप्यति॥211॥

The gambler continuously plays on, even at night, by lamp-light and even when the mother is dead. And gets angry, if questioned in difficulties.

तस्मात् कोपं च कामं च व्यसनारम्भमात्मवान्।
परित्यजेन्मूलहरं वृद्धसेवी जितेन्द्रियः॥212॥

One with character should give up anger and lust, from which all evils start and which destroy the root of life and attain control over senses by serving elders.

यतो निमित्त व्यसनं प्रकृतीनामवाप्नुयात्
प्रागेव प्रतिकुर्वीत तन्निमित्तमतन्द्रितः॥213॥

When factors contributing to trouble for loyal elements arise, immediately these should be countered by suitable measures.

राज्यकारणाद्धि पिता पुत्रान् पुत्राश्च पितर-
मभिद्रुह्यन्ति, किमङ्ग! पुनरमात्यप्रकृतिः?॥214॥

On account of kingdoms father fights sons and sons go against the father. What then to say about minister folk?

लघ्वपि हि व्यसनं अभियुक्तस्य कृच्छ्रं भवति॥215॥

Even a small trouble becomes very troublesome to one under attack.

आरण्योऽग्निरिव हि दुःखामर्षजं तेजो विक्रमयति॥216॥

Like forest fire, the power born out of sorrow and resentment bestows bravery.

न कञ्चिदवमन्येत सर्वस्य शृणुयान्मतम्
बालस्याप्यर्थवद्वाक्यमुपयुञ्जीत पण्डितः॥217॥

No one should be disrespected. Everyone's opinion shall be heard. The wise one should utilize even a child's sensible word.

स्वधर्मः स्वर्गायानन्त्याय च, तस्यातिक्रमे
लोकः संकरादुच्छिद्येत॥218॥

Performance of one's duty leads to heaven and eternal bliss. By violation of duty and consequent confusion people go to ruin.

एष त्रयीधर्मः चतुर्णां वर्णानां आश्रमाणां च
स्वधर्मस्थापनादौपकारिकः॥219॥

The three Vedas are useful in that they lay down the duties for the four castes and the four stages of life.

स्वधर्म संदधानो हि प्रेत्य चेह च नन्दति॥220॥

One who upholds one's duty is happy in this life and the life hereafter.

धर्मार्थाविरोधेन कामं सेवेत, न निः सुखः स्यात्,
समं वा त्रिवर्गमन्योन्यानुबन्धम्।
एको ह्यत्यासेवितो धर्मार्थकामानामात्मानमितरौ च
पीडयति॥221॥

One should enjoy physical pleasures without

harming right conduct and material wealth. Thus shall he be happy. Equal attention should be given to the three kinds of wealth which are interconnected. Any one of the three: righteousness, material wealth, physical pleasures, if excessively indulged in, harms itself and the other two.

न च अकामः पुरुषोऽस्ति॥222॥

There is no man without desire.

नक्षत्रमतिपृच्छन्तं बालमर्थोऽतिवर्तते।
अर्थोह्यर्थस्य नक्षत्रं किं करिष्यन्ति तारकाः?॥223॥

Wealth will desert the childish man who always consults the stars. Wealth is the (auspicious) star for wealth. What can stars (in the sky) do?

शास्त्रविदहष्टकर्मा कर्मसु विषादं गच्छेत्॥224॥

A person with (theoretical) knowledge, but without practical experience, comes to grief in the accomplishment of tasks.

कार्यसामर्थ्याद्धि पुरुषसामर्थ्यं कल्प्यते॥225॥

From the skill exhibited in performance is a man's capacity assessed.

इन्द्रस्य हि स प्रणमति यो बलीयसो नमति॥226॥

He who bows to the powerful bows to Indra (the granter of boons).

स्थिरकर्मा नासमाप्य कर्मोपरमते॥227॥

A steadfast worker does not give up his task without completion.

काष्ठं ह्यग्निरवहितो वसति॥228॥

Fire lurks in wood.

From Chanakya Rajaniti

वाणिज्ये वसते लक्ष्मीस्तदर्ध कृषिकर्मणि।
तदर्थं राजसेवायां भिक्षायां नैव नैव च॥163॥

Prosperity lies in trade (fully), in half measure in agriculture, one fourth in service with the ruler and not at all in begging.

प्रथमे कृषिवाणिज्यं द्वितीये चाश्वपोषणम्।
तृतीये क्रयविक्रयौ चतुर्थे राजसेवनम्॥164॥

First comes agriculture and trade, second rearing horses, third buying and selling and fourth service of the ruler.

स्व्यमुपस्थितं नावमन्येत, स्वयमारूढा हि
स्त्री त्यज्यमानाभिशपतीति लोक प्रवादः॥229॥

What has come of its own shall not be discarded. A woman who makes love on her own, if rejected, showers curses, so goes the saying among the people.

रक्षेदात्मानपात्मवान्॥230॥

The self-controlled one should protect himself.

रक्ष्यः स्वेभ्यः परेभ्यश्च नियमात्मा विपश्चिता॥231॥

The farsighted one should protect himself from both his own people and outsiders.

व्यवस्थितायंमर्यादः कृतवर्णाश्रमस्थितिः।
त्रय्या हि रक्षितो लोकः प्रसीदति न सीदति॥232॥

People rooted in established noble conducts of life, firmly following the prescribed division of duties and the various stages of life, protected by the three Vesas progress and do not decay.

शमव्यायामौ योगक्षेमयोर्योनिः॥233॥

Peace and activity (industry) are the source of security and welfare.

परस्पराधका हि शक्तिदेशकालाः॥234॥

Power, place and time mutually help.

यस्यार्थास्तस्य मित्राणि यस्यार्थास्तस्य बान्धवाः।
यस्यार्थाः स पुमान् लोके यस्यार्थाः स हि पण्डितः॥45॥

He who has wealth has friends, relatives, he counts in the world as a person and is deemed a scholar.

यस्यास्ति वित्तं स नरः कुलीनः
स पण्डितः स श्रुतवान् गुणज्ञः।
स एव वक्ता स च दर्शनीयः
सर्वे गुणाः काञ्चनमाश्रयन्ति॥46॥

He who has wealth is deemed noble, scholar, proficient in scriptures, discerner of qualities, eloquent speaker, and attractive to look at. All qualities are dependent on wealth.

धनं जातिर्धनं रूपं धनं विद्या धन यशः।
किं धनेन विहीनानां याञ्चातिर्जीवितैर्गुणैः॥47॥

Wealth is caste, wealth is learning, wealth is fame, what can those deprived of wealth (and hence of life and qualities) aspire for?

रूपं वश्यैर्बलं भृत्यरुत्तमं मानभर्थिमिः।
महाकुलविवाहैश्च कुलं क्रीणाति वित्तवान्॥48॥

The wealthy one buys beauty with enticements, strength through servants, noble respect through guests, lineage through marriages with big families.

वित्तायत्ताः सदा धर्मा वित्तं कामनिबन्धनम्
वित्तायत्तानि सर्वाणि वित्तं जीवित वर्धनम्॥49॥

All virtues are ever dependent on wealth, wealth captures pleasures, everything is dependent on wealth. Wealth enriches and enhances life.

गुणा धनेन लभ्यन्ते न धनं लभ्यते गुणैः।
धनी गुणवतां सेव्यो न गुणो धनिनां क्वचित्॥51॥

Qualities are attained by wealth, not wealth by qualities, the wealthy one is served by one with good qualities, not vice-versa.

धनं रूपमवैक्लव्यं धनं कुलं सुमङ्गलम्।
धनं यौवनमम्लानं धनमायुर्निरामयम्॥50॥

Wealth is unbewildered beauty, wealth is auspicious family, wealth is unfaded youth, wealth is lasting life.

वृद्धः प्रसिद्धो विबुधो विदग्धः
शूरः श्रुतिज्ञः कवयः कुलीनाः।
विलोकयन्तः सधनस्य वक्त्रं
जयेति जीवेति सदा वदन्ति॥52॥

The old, the famous, the learned, the skilled, the valorous, the one versed in scriptures, noble men all look at the rich man's face and say: "May you be victorious! May you live long!"

स्वगृहेऽपि दरिद्राणां विचक्रुः कचकर्कशम्।
धनिनां परलोकेऽपि प्रेम्णः स्निग्धजना भुवः॥53॥

The poor are loathed in their own homes, the rich have affectionate relatives even in the other world.

कुत आरभ्य घटते विघटय क्वापि गच्छति।
गतिर्न शक्यते ज्ञातुं धनस्य च धनस्य च॥54॥

From where does it come? Where does it go? It is impossible to know the path of wealth.

धनिन सुखिनो नित्यं निर्धना दुःखभागिनः।
धनिनां निर्धनानां च विभागाः सुखदुःखयोः॥55॥

The rich are ever happy, the poor are ever sad, happiness and sorrow are divided among the rich and the poor.

अर्थेन हि विहीनस्य पुरुषस्याल्पमेधसः
विच्छिद्यन्ते क्रियाः सर्वा ग्रीष्मे कुसरितो यथा॥56॥

All actions of one devoid of wealth and of poor retentivity go awry, like the bad river in summer.

पुनर्दाराः पुनर्वित्तं पुनर्मित्रं पुनः सुताः।
पुनरत्रर प्रधानत्वं न शरीरं पुनः पुनः॥98॥

One can regain wife, wealth, friend, children, importance, but not a body.

अन्नहीनो दहेद् राष्ट्र मन्त्रहीनश्च ऋत्विजः।
यजमानं दानहीनो नास्ति यज्ञसमो रिपुः॥99॥

A sacrificial rite without the giving of food and the chanting of mantras destroys the country and without donations destroys the master. There is no enemy like a sacrificial rite.

नास्ति भार्या कुतः शाला धनं नास्ति कुतः सुखम्।
नास्ति भूमिः कुतः सस्यं नास्ति ग्रामः कुतः सीमा॥100॥

If there is no wife, where is the home? If there is no wealth, where is happiness? If there is no land, where is foliage? If there is no village, where is the question of a boundary?

धनिकः श्रोत्रियो राजा नदी वैद्यस्तु पञ्चमः।
पञ्च यत्र न विद्यन्ते न तत्र दिवसं वसेत्॥101॥

One should not stay even for a day at a place where the five do not exist: the rich man, the priest, the ruler, river and the doctor.

पञ्च यत्र न विद्यन्ते न कुर्यात् तत्र संस्थितिम्।
लोक यात्रा भयं लज्जा दाक्षिण्यं धर्मशीलता॥102॥

One should not stay where the five do not exist: means of livelihood, security, sense of shame, courtesy and philanthropy.

यस्मिन् देशे न संमानो न वृर्त्तिन च बान्धवाः।
न च विद्यागमः कश्चित् तं देशं परविर्जयेत्॥103॥

One should avoid the country where there is no reward for work, no activity, no relatives or no means for learning.

कुदेशं च कुवृत्तिं च कुभार्यां कुनदीं तथा।
कुद्रव्यं च कुभोज्यं च वर्जयेच्च विचक्षणः॥107॥

The discerning one should give up a bad country, bad livelihood, bad wife, bad river, bad wealth, bad food.

कुदेशश्च कुवृत्तिश्च कुभार्या कुनदी तथा।
कुमित्रं च कुभोज्यं च वर्जितं पण्डितैः सदा॥108॥

Learned ones should give up bad country, bad livelihood, bad wife, bad river, bad friend and bad food.

कुभार्यां च कुदेशं च कुराजानं कुसौहृदम्।
कुबन्धुं च कुमित्रं च दूरतः परिवर्जयेत्॥109॥

One should avoid at a distance: bad wife, bad country, bad ruler, bad friend, bad relative.

कुदेशमासाद्य कुतोऽर्थसंचयः
कुपुत्रमासाद्य कुतो जलाञ्जलिः
कुगेहिनीं प्राप्य कुतो गृहे सुखं
कुशिष्यमध्यापयतः कुतो यशः॥110॥

On getting a bad country, where is the question of amassing riches? On getting a bad son, how can one get water offering? Where is happiness in the house on getting a bad wife? Where is the scope for fame on getting a bad student?

आतुरे व्यसने प्राप्ते दुर्भिक्षे शत्रु संकटे।
राजद्वारे श्मशाने च यस्तिष्ठति स बान्धवः॥111॥

He is the friend who stands by in illness, adversity, famine, attack by enemy, at the ruler's door and the cremation ground.

परोक्षे कार्यहन्तारं प्रत्यक्षे प्रियवादिनम्।
वर्जयेत् तादृशं मित्रं विषकुम्भं पयोमुखम्॥112॥

One should avoid a friend who speaks sweetly in one's presence and acts against one behind one's back. Such a friend is like a pitcher full of poison, with milk at the surface.

संगतिः श्रयसो मूलं सुजनेषु विशेषतः।
तुषमात्रे पृथग्भिन्ने तण्डुलं न प्ररोहति॥113॥

Alliance with good people is conducive to prosperity (not with bad ones). The grain separated from the husk does not get beaten.

शत्रोरपि गुणा वाच्या दोषा वाच्या गुरोरपि।
युक्तियुक्तं वचो ग्राह्यं न वचो गुरुगौरवात्॥114॥

The good qualities of even an enemy should be spoken, as also the bad qualities of even a teacher. Logically spoken words should be grasped, not everything out of respect of the teacher.

न विश्वसेद विश्वस्ते विश्वस्ते नातिविश्वसेत्।
विश्वासाद् भयमुत्पन्नं मूलान्यपि निकृन्तति॥118॥

One who does not trust us should not be trusted, even the trustworthy should not be trusted too much. Insecurity born out of trust can destroy even the roots.

व्याधिशेषोऽग्निशेषश्च शत्रोः शेष ऋणस्य च।
पुनः पुनः प्रवर्तेत तस्मान्निः शेषमाचरेत्॥119॥

The remnants of an enemy can become active like those of a disease, fire and debt. Hence these should be exterminated completely.

नोपेक्षितव्यो विद्वद्भिः शत्रु रल्पबलोपि सन्।
वह्निरल्पोपि संवृद्धो भस्मसात् कुरुते वनम्॥120॥

Even a weak enemy should not be ignored by wise men, even a weak fire can burn up a forest.

क्षुद्रशत्रुरिति ज्ञात्वा नोपेक्षेत कदाचन।
काले दुर्जनतां याति तृणस्यं वह्निबीजवत्॥121॥

One should never ignore an enemy, knowing him to be weak. He becomes dangerous in due course, like the spark of fire in a haystack.

शत्रोरपत्यानि वशं गतानि
नोपेक्षणीयानि बुधैर्मनुष्यैः।
नान्येव कालेन विपत्कराणि
बनासिपत्रादपि दारुणानि॥122॥

Even the children of enemies who have surrendered should not be ignored by wise men. They will prove dangerous in due course. Wild fires break out even from dry leaves of forest trees.

उपायेन हि यच्छक्यं न तच्छक्यं पराक्रमैः।
काकी कनक सूत्रेण कालसर्पो निपातितः॥123॥

What is not possible by deployment of force is possible by the use of stratagem. The black cobra was defeated by the stratagem of the crow and the golden chain.

नात्यन्तसरलैर्भाव्यं गत्वा पश्य वनस्थलीम्।
छिद्यन्ते सरलास्तत्र कुब्जास्तिष्ठन्ति पादपाः॥124॥

One should not be too straightforward. Go and see the forest. The straight trees are cut down, the crooked ones are left standing.

जिह्वाग्रे वसते लक्ष्मीर्जिह्वाग्रे मित्रबान्धवाः।
जिह्वाग्रे बन्धनं चापि जिह्वाग्रे मरणं ध्रुवम्॥125॥

On the tip of the tongue lives the goddess of prosperity, on the tip of the tongue lie friends and relatives. Imprisonment and death also definitely depend on the tip of the tongue. (Sweetness of speech is very important.)

हे जिह्वे कटुकस्नेहे मधुरं किं न भाषसे।
मधुरं वद कल्याणि लोकोऽयं मधुर प्रियः॥126॥

O tongue, you are fond of pungent things. Why don't you speak sweetly? Speak sweetly, then you will bring prosperity. The world is fond of sweetness.

दुस्तरः सागरस्तीर्णः समूढं वानरं बलम्।
अभूतपूर्वं रामेण सेतुर्बद्धश्च सागरे॥142॥

It is difficult to cross the wide ocean. The army of monkeys was dull witted. Yet strangely, Rama built the bridge in the ocean (with their help).

कार्यार्थी संगतिं याति कृतार्थे नास्ति संगतिः।
तस्मात् सर्वाणि कार्याणि सावशेषाणि कारयेत्॥143॥

Only those with objects in view enter into alliances. There are to be no alliances with people who are satisfied and have no desires to be fulfilled. Hence all tasks should be kept unfinished (in the matter of satisfying allies).

ऐश्वर्यात् सह सम्बन्धं न कुर्याच्च कदाचन।
गते च गौरवं नास्ति आगते च धनक्षयः॥144॥

Alliances should not be concluded for the sake of money or position. When these are lost, the alliance fails.

एको हि दोषो गुणसन्निपाते निमज्जतीन्दोः
किरणेष्विषांकः
केनापि नूनं कविना न दृष्टं दारिद्र यमेकं
गुणराशिनाशि॥59॥

There is only one defect that destroys good fortune: poverty, like the stain in the moon bathed in its rays. (None other has been sighted by the poets.)

चण्डालश्च दरिद्रश्च द्वाविमौ तुलया धृतौ।
एकः स्वबन्धुभिः स्पृष्टस्नैरपि त्यज्यतेऽपरः॥60॥

The pariah and the poor one are even in scales, except that one is touched at least by relatives, whereas the other is abandoned even by them.

त्यजन्ति मित्राणि धनैर्विहीनं पुत्राश्च दाराश्च सुहृज्जनाश्च
नमर्थवन्तं पुनराश्रयन्तेऽप्यर्थों हि लोके पुरुषस्य बन्धुः॥57॥

Friends, sons, wife, relatives all desert the one devoid of wealth, they all return when he becomes rich. Wealth is the real friend of a man in this world.

यत्रोदकं तत्र चरन्ति हंसास्तदेव शुष्कं परिवर्जयन्ति।
प्राप्ते जले तत् पुनराश्रयन्ते न हंसमित्रेण नरेण
भाव्यम्॥58॥

Swans stay at a place when there is water. They abandon it when it dries up and come back when there is again water. Man should not be like swans.

लुब्धमर्थेन गृह्लीयात् स्तब्धमञ्जलिकर्मणा।
मूर्खं छन्दोऽनुवृत्तेन याथार्थ्येन च पण्डितम्॥145॥

The miser should be won over by means of wealth, the proud man by offering respect, the fool by flattery, and the learned one by truthfulness.

उत्तम प्रणिपातेन शूरं भेदेन योजयेत्।
नीचभल्पप्रदानेन समशक्तिं पराक्रमैः॥146॥

The superior one should be dealt with by submission, the valiant one by division, the low one by gifts and the equal by prowess.

त्यजेत् धर्म दाहीनं विद्याहीनं गुरु त्यजेत्।
त्यजेत् क्रोधमुखीं भार्यां निःस्नेहान् बान्धवांस्त्यजेत्॥147॥

Ruthless law, teacher without learning, wife with an angry face and relatives without affection should be given up.

विद्यार्थी सेवकः पान्थाः क्षुधार्तो भयकातरः।
भाण्डारी प्रतिहारी च सप्त सुप्तान् प्रबोधयेत्॥249॥

Seven sleeping ones should be woken up: the treasurer, doorkeeper, the student, the servant, the traveller, the hungry one and the one who is afraid.

निरालस्याः सुसंतुष्टाः सुस्वप्नाः सुप्रबोधिनः।
सुखदुःखसमा धीरा भृत्या जगति दुर्लभाः॥191॥

Servants who are not lazy, who are satisfied, who have good aspirations, who are vigilant, who are alike in happiness and sorrow, and who are brave are rare in this world.

वसन्ति नगरे देवास्तथा ग्रामेऽधमा जना
ग्रामान्तरे पिशचाश्च ग्रामामध्ये तु राक्षसाः॥251॥

The elite live in cities, the lowly in villages, the devils in between villages and demons in the midst of villages.

पण्डितेषु गुणाः सर्वे मूर्खे दोषाश्च केवलम्।
तस्मान्मूर्खसहस्रेषु प्राज्ञ एको विशिष्यते॥198॥

A wise man has only good qualities, a fool only bad ones. Hence a single wise man is better than a thousand fools.

गुणवन्तं नियुञ्जीत गुणहीनं विवर्जयेत्।
पण्डिते च गुणाः सर्वे मूर्खे दोषाश्च केवलाः॥199॥

The one with good qualities should be employed and the one without them avoided. The wise man has all good qualities while the fool has only faults.

वामा भार्या सुतो मूर्खः प्रेषकोऽवाग्विचारकः।
निःस्नेहो बन्धु वर्गश्च त्यजेदस्य महत्सुखम्॥187॥

He attains great happiness who gives up an adverse wife, idiotic son, a non-eloquent envoy and relatives who are not affectionate.

कुनयं मन्त्रिराजानां विप्रं च वृषलीपतिम्।
प्रव्राजिनं व्रतभ्रष्टं न सेवन्ति सदा बुधाः॥188॥

Wise men never serve rulers guided by ministers along wrong paths, a Brahmin who has married a sudra wife, and the ascetic who has violated his vows.

नवं वस्त्रं नवं छत्रं वनानां च नवं फलम्।
सर्वं नवं प्रशंसीयात् सेवकं च पुरातनम्॥172॥

One should praise new clothes, new umbrella, new fruits in the forest and all new things, but only an old servant.

त्यजेत् स्वामिनमत्युग्रमत्युग्रात् कृपणं त्यजेत्।
कृपणादविशेषज्ञं तस्माच्च कृतनाशनम्॥173॥

One should give up a cruel master, more so a miserly one, an indiscriminate one more than a miser, and an ungrateful one first of all.

देवताः पूजयेद् भक्त्या भृत्यान् दानेन पूजयेत्।
उपकारेण शूद्रं च विप्रं प्रणतिवन्दनात्॥165॥

Gods should be propitiated with devotion, servants with gifts, labour class with favours and the Brahmin with show of respect.

कुग्रामवासः कुलहीनसेवा कुभोजनं क्रोधमुखी च भार्या।
पुत्रश्च मूर्खो विधवा च कन्या विनाग्निना षट् प्रदहन्ति कायम्॥169॥

Six things burn the body without the aid of fire: living in a bad village, serving a bad ruling family, bad food, short-tempered wife, idiotic son, widowed daughter.

भृत्या बहुविधा ज्ञेया उत्तमाधममध्यमाः।
ते नियोज्या यथायोग्यं त्रिविधेष्वेवकर्मसु॥189॥

Servants are known to be superior, bad and mediocre. They should be assigned various duties according to their capacities.

दुर्जनस्य च सर्पस्य वरं सर्पो न दुर्जनः।
सर्पो दशति कालेन दुर्जनस्तु पदे पदे॥195॥

Between a serpent and an evil man, the serpent is preferable. The serpent bites occasionally, but the evil man at every step.

स्त्री विनश्यति रूपेण ब्राह्मणो राजसेवया।
गावो दूरप्रचारेणं हिरण्यं लाभलिप्सया॥171॥

A woman comes to ruin through her beauty, the Brahmin by serving the ruler, cattle by straying far and money is lost by excessive greed for profit.

प्रलये भिन्नमर्यादा भवन्ति सागराः।
सागरा भेद मिच्छन्ति प्रलयेऽपि न साधवः॥197॥

At the time of deluge, oceans exceed their limits,

but good people never.

यथा चतुर्भिः कनकं परीक्ष्यते निघर्षणच्छेदनतापताडनैः।
तथा चतुर्भिः पुरुषः परीक्ष्यते कुलेन शीलेन गुणेन कर्मणा॥192॥

A man is tested in four ways: with reference to his family, conduct, quality and action, just as gold is tested in four ways: by scratching, breaking, heating and beating.

यथा हेम परीक्षेत तापताडनच्छेदनैः।
तथा पुरुषमप्येवं कुलशीलेन कर्मणा॥193॥

Just as gold is tested by heating, beating and breaking, so a person is tested by family, conduct and action.

जानीयात् प्रेषणे भृत्यान् बान्धवान् व्यसनागमे।
मित्रं चापत्तिकालेषु भार्यां च विभवक्षये॥194॥

Servants can be known when sent on errands, relatives when difficulties arise, a friend in times of distress, and the wife when prosperity declines.

गणितज्ञो लिपेर्वक्ता श्रुतिस्मृतिपरायणः।
ब्राह्मणो ग्रहमन्त्रज्ञो देववत् सोऽपि राध्यकः॥225॥

The Brahmin who knows mathematics, interprets scripts, is interested in the ancient scriptures and is able to interpret the secrets of planets is worthy of worship like a god.

कान्तावियोगः स्वजनापमान ऋणस्य शेषं कुनृपस्य सेवा।
दरिद्रभावाद् विमुखं च मित्रं विनाग्निना पञ्च दहन्ति
कायम्॥168॥

Five things burn the body without the aid of fire: serving a bad ruler, uncleared debt, disgrace of one's people, separation from beloved, a friend who turns his face away because one is poor.

पितृपैतामहोदक्षः शास्त्रज्ञो मिपृपाचकः।
सत्यशौचसमायुक्तः सूपकारः स उच्यते॥227॥

The royal cook is he who has inherited skill from his father and grandfather, knows the culinary art well and cooks tasty food, and is clean and honest.

विषं चङ्क्रमणं रात्रौ विषं राज्ञोऽनुकूलता
विषं स्त्रियोऽप्यन्यहृदो विषं व्याधिरवीक्षितः॥81॥

Wandering at night is poison, pleasure of the ruler is poison, women whose hearts are lost to others are poison, disease undetected is poison.

सद्भिरासीत सततं सद्भिः कुर्वीत संगतिम्।
सद्भिर्विवादं मैत्रीं च नासद्भिः किं चिदाचरेत्॥82॥

(The ruler) should sit with good people, keep company with them, discuss with them and be friendly with them, not with bad people.

चापलाद् वारयेद् दृष्टिं मिथ्यावाक्यं च वारयेत्।
मानवे श्रोत्रिये चैव भृत्यवर्गे सदैव हि॥79॥

One should ever guard against fickleness and falsehood in men, priests and servant class.

वित्तेन रक्ष्यते धर्मो विद्या योगेन रक्ष्यते।
मृदुना रक्ष्यते भूपः सत्स्त्रिया रक्ष्यते गृहम्॥80॥

Righteousness is protected by wealth, learning by practice, the ruler by gentleness, the home by a good woman.

पण्डितैश्च विनीतैश्च धर्मज्ञैः सत्यवादिभिः
बन्धनेऽपि वसेत् सार्धं न तु राज्ये खलैः सह॥83॥

One should stay with scholars, humble ones, those who know the righteous path, and those who speak the truth even in prison, but not with evil ones in a state.

एकं चक्षुर्विवेको हि द्वितीयं सत्समागमः।
तौ न स्तो यस्य स क्षिप्रं मोहकूपे पतेद् ध्रुवम्॥84॥

One eye is discerning judgement, the other is the company of good people. He who does not have these two eyes falls fast into the well of delusion.

अरि मित्रमुदासीनं मध्यस्थं स्थविरं गरुम्।
यो न बुध्यति मन्दात्मा स च सर्वत्र नश्यति॥85॥

That dull-headed person who cannot discern a foe, friend, a lazy one, a mediator, an old man, a teacher perishes everywhere.

भ्रमन् संपूज्यते राजा भ्रमन् संपूज्यते द्विजः
भ्रमन् संपूज्यते योगो स्त्री भ्रमन्ती विनश्यति॥86॥

The ruler who moves about is venerated, as also the Brahmin and the yogi who travel, but a woman who wanders gets destroyed.

अविद्यः पुरुषः शोच्यः शोच्यं मैथुनमप्रजम्।
निराहाराः प्रजाः शोच्याः शोच्यं राज्यमराजकम्॥95॥

An unruly country is to be pitied, like an illiterate person, unproductive copulation and foodless people.

धन्यास्ते ये न पश्यन्ति देशभङ्गं कुलक्षयम्।
परचित्तगतां नारीं पुत्रं च व्यसने स्थितम्॥96॥

Blessed are they who do not live to see the ruin of one's country, the decay of family, a woman gone astray and a son in difficulties.

पुनर्वित्तं पुनर्मित्रं पुनर्भार्या पुनर्मही।
एतत् सर्वं पुनर्लभ्यं न शरीरं पुनः पुनः॥97॥

One can regain wealth, friend, wife, kingdom, but not a body.

पठ पुत्रर किमालस्यमपठो भारवाहकः
पठंस्तु पूजितो राज्ञा पठ पुत्र दिने दिने॥70॥

Read, son, read. Why be lazy? The illiterate is a burden-carrier. The scholar is venerated by the ruler. Read son every day.

ऐश्वर्यमध्रुवं प्राप्य ध्रुवधर्मे मतिं कुरु।
क्षणादेव विनाशिन्यः सम्पदोऽप्यात्मना सह॥43॥

After amassing riches (which are impermanent), turn your mind to righteousness (which is permanent). Riches perish along with oneself in a moment.

ऊर्ध्वं न क्षीरविच्छेदात् पयो धेनोरबाप्यते।
एवं राष्ट्रादयोगेन पीड़ितान्नाप्यते बलिः॥63॥

Milk is not obtained by drying up the cow. Similarly from the country fruits are obtained by proper tapping and not by harassment.

3
People and Precepts

From Chanakya Sutras

लुब्धसेवी पावकेच्छया खद्योतं धमति॥282॥

One who serves a miserly master is like one who fans the firefly to get fire.

विशेषज्ञं स्वामिनमाश्रयेत्॥283॥

One should serve a learned master.

पुरुषस्य मैथुनं जरा॥284॥

Excessive sex ages men.

स्त्रीणाममैथुनं जरा॥285॥

Lack of sex ages women.

न नीचोत्तमयोर्वैवाहः॥286॥

There can be no marriage between the high and the low.

अगम्यागमनादायुर्यशःपुण्यानि क्षीयन्ते॥287॥

Association with low (characterless) women reduces life-span, reputation and virtue.

नास्त्यहंकारसमः शत्रुः॥288॥

There is no enemy equal to arrogance.

ससदि शत्रुं न परिक्रोशेत्॥289॥

In an assembly, an enemy should not be criticised.

शत्रुव्यसनं श्रवणसुखम्॥290॥

An enemy's trouble is pleasant to hear.

समकाले स्वयमपि प्रभुत्वस्य प्रयोजनं भवति॥273॥

At the appropriate time, prosperity is useful.

नीचस्य विद्याः पापकर्मणि योजयन्ति॥274॥

Learning of the low-minded is yoked to sinful deeds.

पयःपानमपि विषवर्धनं भुजंगस्य नामृतं स्यात्॥275॥

Feeding a snake with milk increases its venom, no nectar is produced.

न हि धान्यसमो ह्यर्थः॥276॥

No other wealth can equal grain.

न क्षुधासमः शत्रुः॥277॥

There is no enemy equal to hunger.

अकृतेर्नियता क्षुत्॥278॥

One who does wrong things has to inevitably suffer hunger.

नास्त्यभक्ष्यं क्षुधितस्य॥279॥

There is nothing uneatable for a hungry one.

इन्द्रियाणि जरावशं कुर्वन्ति॥280॥

Over-indulgence in senses ages one fast.

सानुक्रोशं भर्तारमाजीवेत्॥281॥

One should earn one's livelihood, serving a compassionate master.

न कृतार्थानां मरणभयम॥264॥

The contented have no fear of death.

कस्यचिदर्थं स्वमिव मन्यते साधुः॥265॥

The good one considers others' wealth as his own.

परविभवेष्वादरो न कर्त्तव्यः॥266॥

One should not be desirous of others' prosperity.

परविभवेष्वादरोऽपि नाशमूलम्॥267॥

Desire for others' prosperity is the root of destruction.

पलालमपि परद्रव्यं न हर्तव्यम्॥268॥

Another's wealth, even if it be husk, should not be stolen.

परद्रव्यापहरणमात्मद्रव्यनाशहेतुः॥269॥

Stealing others' wealth leads to loss of one's own.

न चौर्यात्परं मृतयुपाशः॥270॥

There is no greater bond to sorrow than stealing.

यवागूरपि प्राणधारणं करोति काले॥271॥

Even gruel, obtained in time, helps maintain life.

न मृतस्यौपधं प्रयोजनम्॥272॥

To the dead, medicine is of no use.

महेन्द्रमप्यर्थहीनं न बहु मन्यते लोकः॥256॥

The world does not respect one without riches, even if he be Indra (the king of gods).

दारिद्रयं खलु पुरुषस्य जीवितं मरणम्॥257॥

Poverty is death, while living.

विरूपोऽर्थवान् सुरूपः॥258॥

Even an ugly one, if rich, is considered handsome.

अदातारमप्यर्थवन्तमर्थिनो न त्यजन्ति॥259॥

The aid-seekers do not give up the rich one, even if

he be not a donor.

अकुलीनोऽपि धनी कुलीनाद्विशिष्टः।।260।।

Even a low born, if rich, will be deemed superior to the high born.

नास्त्यवमानभयमनार्यस्य।।261।।

The ignoble have no fear of shame.

न चेतनवतां वृत्तिभयम्।।262।।

The intelligent have no fear about their livelihood.

न जितेन्द्रियाणां विषयभयम्।।263।।

Those who have controlled their senses are not afraid of sensual objects.

माताऽपि दुष्टा त्याज्या।।247।।

Even a mother, if cruel, has to be given up.

स्वहस्तोऽपि विषदिग्धश्छेद्यः।।248।।

One's own hand, if poisoned, has to be cut off.

परोऽपि च हितो बन्धुः।।249।।

A benefactor, even if he be a foreigner, is a kinsman.

कक्षादप्यौषधं गृह्यते।।250।।

Medicine can be extracted even from dry grass.

नास्ति चौरेपु विश्वासः।।251।।

Thieves should not be trusted.

अप्रतीकारेष्वनादरो न कर्त्तव्यः।।252।।

Easy tasks should not be neglected.

व्यसनं मनागपि बाधते॥253॥

Even a small weakness creates trouble.

अमरवदर्थजातमर्जयेत्॥254॥

One should earn wealth as if one is immortal.

अर्थवान् सर्वलोकस्य बहुमतः॥255॥

The wealthy are respected by all.

धर्मेण जयतिं लोकान्॥238॥

One can conquer the worlds with righteousness.

मृत्युरपि धर्मिष्ठं रक्षति॥239॥

Even death protects the righteous.

धर्माद्विपरीतं पापं यत्र प्रसज्यते तत्र धर्मावमतिर्महती प्रसज्यते॥240॥

Where a sinful act contrary to righteousness is propagated, great disregard of righteousness is propagated.

उपस्थितविनाशानां प्रकृत्या कारेण कार्येण लक्ष्यते॥241॥

The state of those about to perish is seen through their appearance and deeds.

आत्मविनाशं सूचययधर्मबुद्धिः॥242॥

The evil intellect suggests self-destruction.

पिशुनवादिनो न रहस्यम्॥243॥

Slander mongers will not keep secrets.

पररहस्यं नैव श्रोतव्यम्॥244॥

Don't listen to others' secrets.

वल्लभस्य कारकत्वमधर्मयुक्तम्॥245॥

It is not proper for a ruler to be an agent.

स्वजनेष्वतिक्रमो न कर्त्तव्यः॥246॥

One should not disrespect one's people.

मूर्खस्तु परिहर्तव्यः प्रत्यक्षो क्षिपदः पशुः।
भिनत्ति वाक्यशल्येन अदृष्टः कण्टको यथा॥207॥

A fool should be avoided, he is a two-footed animal. He hurts with sharp words like an unseen thorn.

बहुभिर्मूर्खसंघातैरन्योन्य पशुवृत्तिभिः।
प्रच्छाद्यन्ते गुणाः सर्वे मेघैरिव दिवाकरः॥208॥

All good qualities get hidden, by surrounding oneself with groups of fools who act like animals, as the sun is hidden by clouds.

उपस्थितविनाशः पथ्यवाक्यं न शृणोति॥395॥

The one for whom destruction is imminent does not listen to wholesome advice.

नास्ति देहिनां सुखदुःखाभावः॥396॥

There is no escape from pleasure and pain for embodied beings.

मातरमिव वत्साः सुखदुःखानि कर्तारमेवानुगच्छन्ति॥397॥

Like children their mother, pleasure and pain follow the doer (of actions).

तिलमात्रमप्युपकारं शैलवन्मन्यते साधुः॥398॥

The good one considers even a tiny help rendered to him as very big.

उपकारोऽनार्येष्वकर्त्तव्यः॥399॥

Evil ones should not be helped.

प्रत्युपकारभयादनार्यः शत्रुर्भवति॥400॥

Out of fear that help received has to be repaid, the low-minded one becomes an enemy.

स्वल्पमप्युपकारकृते प्रत्युपकार कर्तुमार्यो न स्वपिति॥401॥

The noble one does not forget to render great help in return for the smallest aid received.

श्रुतिसुखात् कोकिलालापात् तुष्यन्ति॥446॥

Words should be spoken which delight the ear like koel's cooing.

स्वधर्महेतुः सत्पुरुषः॥447॥

A man who does his duty is a good and righteous man.

नास्त्यर्थिनो गौरवम्॥448॥

Beggars cannot have dignity.

स्त्रीणां भूषणं सौभाग्यम्॥449॥

Husband is a woman's ornament.

शत्रोरपि न पातनीया वृत्तिः॥450॥

Even an enemy should not be deprived of his livelihood.

अप्रयत्नोदकं क्षेत्रम्॥451॥

The land where water is easily available is the right field to be cultivated.

एरण्डमवलम्ब्य कुञ्जरं न कोपयेत्॥452॥

One should not anger the elephant with the support of the castor plant. (One should not anger the mighty with the support of the weak.)

अतिप्रवृद्धा शाल्मली वारणस्तम्भो न भवति॥453॥

Even if well-grown, the silk-cotton tree does not become a fit pillar to bind an elephant.

अशुभद्वेषिणः स्त्रीषु न प्रसक्ताः॥480॥

Enemies of evil are not addicted to women.

यज्ञफलज्ञास्त्रिवेदविदः॥481॥

Those who are well-versed in the three Vedas know the results of sacrifices.

स्वर्गस्थानं न शाश्वतं यावत् पुण्यफलम्॥482॥

Stay in heaven is not permanent, it lasts only till the reserves of accumulated virtue remain.

न च स्वर्गपतनात् परं दुःखम्॥483॥

To fall from heaven is the greatest sorrow.

देही देहं त्यक्त्वा ऐन्द्रं पदं न वाञ्छति॥484॥

The embodied one does not desire even the status of Indra (heavenly rule), if the body has to be given up.

दुःखानामौषधं निर्वाणम्॥485॥

Liberation is the remedy for all sorrows.

अनार्यसम्बन्धाद्वरमार्यशत्रुता॥486॥

Enmity of the noble is better than alliance with the ignoble.

निहन्ति दुर्वचनं कुलम्॥487॥

Bad language destroys the family.

न पुत्रसंस्पर्शात् परं सुखम्॥488॥

No pleasure is greater than the touch of one's children.

विवादे धर्ममनुस्मरेत्॥489॥

In debate, what is right should be remembered.

निशान्ते कार्यं चिन्तयेत्॥490॥

Every morning, the day's tasks should be planned.

प्रदोषे न संयोगः कर्त्तव्यः॥491॥

At twilight, sex should not be indulged in.

उपस्थित विनाशो दुर्नयं मन्यते॥492॥

He, whose destruction is imminent, plans evil action.

क्षीरार्थिनः किं करिण्या॥493॥

What is the use of an elephant for one in need of milk?

न दानसमं वश्यम्॥494॥

There is no attraction equal to a gift.

परायत्तेषूत्कण्ठां न कुर्यात्॥495॥

One should not desire others' property.

असत्समृद्धिरसद्भिरेव भुज्यते॥496॥

Evil riches are enjoyed by only the evil-minded.

दैवायत्तं न शोचेत्॥524॥

One should not question God's will.

आश्रितदुःखमात्मनं इव मन्यते साधुः॥525॥

The good one considers the sorrow of those who take refuge in him as his own.

हृद्गतमाच्छाद्यान्यद् वदत्यनार्यः॥526॥

The ignoble one hides his real feelings and spcaks

out something else.

बुद्धिहीनः पिशाचतुल्यः॥527॥

The unintelligent are equal to ghosts.

असहायः पथि न गच्छत्॥528॥

One should not travel without an aide.

पुत्रो न स्तोतव्यः॥529॥

One's son should not be praised.

स्वामी स्तोतव्योऽनुजीविभिः॥530॥

The master should be praised by subordinates.

धर्मकृत्येष्वपि स्वामिन एव घोषयेत्॥531॥

Even in the performance of allotted duties, the master should be praised.

राजाज्ञां नातिलंघयेत्॥532॥

The ruler's order should not be disobeyed.

यथा ज्ञप्तं तथा कुर्यात्॥533॥

Whatever has been ordered (by the ruler) should be carried out.

नास्ति बुद्धिमतां शत्रुः॥534॥

The intelligent have no enemies.

आत्मच्छिद्रं न प्रकाशयेत्॥535॥

One's weakness should not be divulged.

क्षमावानेव सर्वं साधयति॥536॥

The patient one achieves everything.

आपदर्थं धनं रक्षेत्॥537॥

Money should be saved for difficult days.

साहसवतां प्रियं कर्त्तव्यम्॥538॥

The daring ones love their duty.

श्वः कार्यमद्य कुर्वीत॥539॥

Tomorrow's deed, do today.

आपराह्निकं पूर्वाह्न एव कर्त्तव्यम्॥540॥

What is to be done in the afternoon should be done in the forenoon.

व्यवहारानुलोमो धर्मः॥541॥

What is right depends on the nature of the case.

सर्वज्ञता लोकज्ञता॥542॥

Experience of the world is all-knowledge.

शास्त्रज्ञोऽप्यलोकज्ञो मूर्खतुल्यः॥543॥

A learned scholar, without world experience, is equal to a fool.

शास्त्रप्रयोजनं तत्त्वदर्शनम्॥544॥

The use of science is the sight of truth.

तत्त्वज्ञानं कार्यमेव प्रकाशयति॥545॥

Knowledge of truth lights up one's deeds.

व्यवहारे पक्षपातो न कार्यः॥546॥

Onc should be impartial in judging cases.

धर्मादपि व्यवहारो गरीयान्॥547॥

Proper behaviour is more important than being virtuous.

आत्मा हि व्यवहारस्य साक्षी॥548॥

The soul is the witness of a transaction.

सर्वसाक्षी ह्यात्मा॥549॥

The spirit (soul) is the witness of everything.

न स्यात् कूटसाक्षी॥550॥

One should not be a false witness.

कूटसाक्षिणो नरके पतन्ति॥551॥

False witnesses fall into hell.

प्रच्छन्नपापानां साक्षिणो महाभूतानि॥552॥

Witnesses of hidden sins are the great elements.

आत्मनः पापमात्मैव प्रकाशयति॥553॥

One's sin is revealed by oneself.

व्यवहारेऽन्तर्गतमाचारः सूचयति॥554॥

In behaviour, the outer form indicates the inner core.

आकारसंवरणं देवानामशक्यम्॥555॥

To hide one's form is impossible even for the gods.

चोरराजपुरुषेभ्यो वित्तं रक्षेत्॥556॥

Wealth should be protected from robbers and ruling officials.

1. Rulers and People

दुर्दर्शना हि राजानः प्रजाः नाशयन्ति॥557॥

Inaccessible rulers destroy the people.

सुदर्शना हि राजानः प्रजा रञ्जयन्ति॥558॥

Easily accessible rulers please the people.

न्याययुक्तं राजानं मातरं मन्यन्ते प्रजाः॥559॥

The people deem a just ruler a mother.

तादृशः स राजा इह सुखं ततः स्वर्गमाप्नोति॥560॥

Such a ruler attains material happiness and later heaven.

2. General Dicta

अहिंसालक्षणो धर्मः॥561॥

Non-violence is the sign of righteousness.

स्वशरीरमपि परशरीरं मन्यते साधुः॥562॥

The good one considers his body as another's.

मांसभक्षणमयुक्तं सर्वेषाम्॥563॥

Meat-eating is improper for everyone.

न संसारभयं ज्ञानवताम्॥564॥

The wise are not afraid of *samsara.*

विज्ञानदीपेन संसारभयं निवर्तते॥565॥

The fear of phenomenal world is rid by the light of knowledge.

सर्वमनित्यं भवति॥566॥

Everything (in the phenomenal world) is transient.

कृमिशकृन्मूत्रभाजनं शरीर पुण्यपापजन्महेतु॥567॥

The body which contains worms and excreta is the creator of virtue and vice.

जन्ममरणादिषु दुःखमेव॥568॥

There is only sorrow in birth and death.

तेभ्यस्तर्तुं प्रयतेत॥569॥

One should try to escape the cycle of births and deaths.

तपसा स्वर्गमाप्नोति॥570॥

Heaven is attained by penance.

क्षमायुक्तस्य तपो विवर्धते॥571॥

The penance of the patient ever grows.

तस्मात् सर्वेषां कार्यसिद्धिर्भवति॥572॥

Through penance, all attain their goals.

गुरुणां माता गरीयसी॥362॥

A mother is the greatest teacher.

सर्वावस्थासु माता भर्तव्या॥363॥

In all circumstances, the mother should be looked after.

वैदुष्यमलंकारेणाच्छाद्यते॥364॥

Wisdom is clothed in figures of speech.

स्त्रीणां भूषणं लज्जा॥365॥

Modesty is the ornament of women.

विप्राणां भूषणं वेदः॥366॥

Knowledge is the ornament of the learned.

सर्वेषां भूषणं धर्मः॥367॥

Righteousness is the ornament of all.

भूषणानां भूषणं सविनया विद्या॥368॥

Learning, accompanied by humility, is the ornament of ornaments.

अनुपद्रवं देशमाबसेत्॥369॥

One should live in a country free from strife.

सर्वाश्च सम्पदः सर्वोपायेन परिग्रहेत्॥114॥

All types of riches should be amassed by all means.

भाग्यवन्तमपरीक्ष्यकारिणं श्रीः परित्यजति॥115॥

Prosperity forsakes even a lucky one if he acts without foresight.

ज्ञानानुमानैश्च परीक्षा कर्त्तव्या॥116॥

Examination (of a thing) should be done with reference to what is known and what is to be inferred.

यो यस्मिन् कर्मणि कुशलस्तं तस्मिन्नेव योजयेत्॥117॥

Everyone should be yoked to the task for which he is befitted.

दुःसाधमपि सुसाधं करोत्युपायज्ञः॥118॥

The one who knows the means makes the impossible possible.

अज्ञानिना कृतमपि न बहु मन्तव्यम्॥119॥

What is done by an unintelligent person should not be rated high.

यादृच्छिकत्वात् कृमिरपि रूपान्तराणि करोति॥120॥

Sometimes, due to fortuitous circumstances even a worm assumes different forms.

सिद्धस्यैव कार्यस्य प्रकाशनं कर्त्तव्यम्॥121॥

Only accomplished deeds should be publicized.

ज्ञानवतामपि दैवमानुषदोषात् कार्याणि दुष्यन्ति॥122॥

Even the affairs of the learned go awry duc to defective destiny and human interference.

व्यालाश्रयापि विफलापि सकण्टकापि
वक्रापि पंकिलाभावापि दुरा सदापि
गन्धेन बन्धुरिह केनकपुष्पवल्ली
एको गुणः खलु निहन्ति समस्तदोषान्॥

Though located in a snake-infested place, bears no fruit, is full of thorns, has crooked leaves and stands in mud, and is unapproachable due to these drawbacks, the Ketaka flower overcomes all these defects with one good quality: its fragrance!

आज्ञाफलमैश्वर्यम्॥211॥

A command (order) (of the ruler) should result in prosperity.

दातव्यमपि बालिशः परिक्लेशेन दास्यति॥212॥

The foolish give what is to be given with great difficulty.

महदैश्वर्यं प्राप्याप्यधृतिमान् विनश्यति॥213॥

Even after attaining great prosperity, the one without fortitude perishes.

नास्त्यधृतेरंहिकामुष्मिकम्॥214॥

The one without fortitude does not enjoy anything either materially or spiritually.

न दुर्जनैः सह संसर्गः कर्त्तव्यः॥215॥

Don't associate with bad people.

शौण्डहस्तगतं पयोऽप्यवमन्येत॥216॥

Even milk in the hands of a drunkard acquires disrepute.

कार्यसंकटेष्वर्थव्यवसायिनी बुद्धि॥217॥

Intellect is that which can decide on action in difficulties.

मितभोजनं स्वास्थ्यम्॥218॥

Moderate eating is healthy.

पथ्यमपथ्यं वाऽजीर्णे नाश्नीयात्॥219॥

In indigestion, no food (wholesome or otherwise) should be taken.

जीर्णभोजिनं व्याधिर्नोपसर्पति॥220॥

Disease does not touch one who digests his food.

जीर्णशरीरे वर्धमानं व्याधि नोपेक्षेत॥221॥

In an old body, a growing disease should not be neglected.

अजीर्णे भोजनं दुःखम्॥222॥

Eating is painful in indigestion.

शत्रोरपि विशिष्यते व्याधिः॥223॥

Disease excels an enemy.

दानं निधानमनुगामि॥224॥

Donation follows wealth.

पटुतरे तृष्णापरे सुलभमतिसन्धानम्॥225॥

It is easy to deceive the clever and the greedy.

तृष्णया मतिश्छाद्यते॥226॥

Greed clouds the intellect.

कार्यबुत्वे बहुफलमायतिकं कुर्यात्॥227॥

When the tasks are great, abundant rewards should be made the incentive.

स्वयमेवावस्कन्न कार्यं निरीक्षेत॥228॥

Secret tasks should be scrutinised by oneself.

मूर्खेषु साहसं नियतम्॥229॥
With fools daring should be controlled.

मूर्खेषु विवादो न कर्त्तव्यः॥230॥
Don't debate with fools.

मूर्खेषु मूर्खवत्कथयेत्॥231॥
Speak like a fool to a fool.

आयसैरायसं छेद्यम्॥232॥
Iron should be cut by iron.

नास्त्यधीमतः सखा॥233॥
The unintelligent have no companions.

धर्मेण धार्यते लोकः॥234॥
The world is borne by righteousness.

प्रेतमपि धर्माधर्मावनुगच्छतः॥235॥
Vice and virtue pursue even the departed spirit.

दया धर्मस्य जन्मभूमि॥236॥
Kindness is the mother of righteousness.

धर्ममूले सत्यदाने॥237॥
Truth and charity are the roots of righteousness.

अधनस्य बुद्धिर्न विद्यते॥291॥
A poor one has no intellect.

हितमप्यधनस्य वाक्यं न गृह्यते॥292॥
A poor man's word, even if apt, is not heard.

अधनः स्वभार्ययाऽप्यवमन्यते॥293॥
The poor one is despised by his own wife.

पुष्पहीन सहकारमपि नोपासते भ्रमराः॥294॥

Bees do not go to the flowerless mango tree.

विद्याधनमधनानाम्॥295॥

Learning is wealth to the poor.

विद्या चौरैरपि न ग्राह्या॥296॥

The wealth of learning cannot be stolen by thieves.

विद्या ख्यापिता ख्यातिः॥297॥

Fame is glorified by learning.

यशःशरीरं न विनश्यति॥298॥

Fame is immortal.

यः परार्थमुपसर्पति स सत्पुरुषः॥299॥

He is the good one who moves forward to help others.

राजदासी न सेवितव्या॥379॥

The king's courtesan should not be courted.

न चक्षुषाऽपि राजानं निरीक्षेत॥380॥

The ruler should not be viewed with lifted eyes.

पुत्रे गुणवति कुटुम्बिनः स्वर्गः॥381॥

When children are good, homes are heaven.

पुत्रा विद्यानां पारं गमयितव्याः॥382॥

Children should be made to reach the shores of knowledge (that is, given maximum education).

जनपदार्थं ग्रामं त्यजेत्॥383॥

For the country's sake, (the interests of) the village should be forsaken.

ग्रामार्थं कुटुम्बस्त्यज्यते॥384॥

For the sake of the village, (the interests of) the family should be forsaken.

अतिलाभः पुत्रलाभः॥385॥

The greatest gain is the gain of a son.

दुर्गतेः पितरौ रक्षति स पुत्रः॥386॥

He who protects from difficulties, is the son.

षट्कर्णाद् भिद्यते मन्त्रः॥34॥

On being heard by six ears, secrecy of counsel gets broken.

3. Allies, Friends

आपत्सु स्नेहसंयुक्तं मित्रम्॥35॥

One who is affectionate in difficulties is the friend.

मित्रसंग्रहणे बलं संपद्यते॥36॥

In the acquisition of allies, one develops strength.

बलवानलब्धलाभे प्रयतते॥37॥

The strong one tries to get what has not been attained.

4. Evils of Laziness

अलब्धलाभी नालसस्य॥38॥

The lazy one does not get what has not been obtained.

अलसस्य लब्धमपि रक्षितुं न शक्यते॥39॥

The lazy one cannot guard even what has been begotten.

न चालसस्य रक्षितं विवर्धते॥40॥

Anything looked after by the lazy does not grow.

न भृत्यान् प्रेषयति॥41॥

(The lazy one) cannot even command servants.

5. State Policy

अलब्धलाभादिचतुष्टयं राज्यतन्त्रम्॥42॥

Getting what has not been got, guarding it, developing it and then distributing it – these four constitute state policy.

स्थान एव नराः पूज्यन्ते॥309॥

Men are respected only in their positions.

आर्यवृत्तमनुतिष्ठेत्॥310॥

One should follow the mode of life of noble men.

कदापि मर्यादां नातिक्रमेत्॥311॥

One should never transgress the bounds of decorum.

नास्त्यर्घ पुरुषरत्नस्य॥312॥

A jewel among men is invaluable.

न स्त्रीरत्नसमं रत्नम्॥313॥

There is no jewel equal to a good woman.

सुदुर्लभं रत्नम्॥314॥

Gems are difficult to obtain.

अयशोभय भयेषु॥315॥

Fear of a bad name is the greatest fear.

नास्त्यलसस्य शास्त्रागमः॥316॥

An idle one cannot learn the sciences.

न स्त्रैणस्य स्वर्गाप्तिर्धर्मकृत्यं च॥317॥

A womanizer does not do righteous deeds, nor does he attain heaven.

धेनोः शीलज्ञः क्षीरं भुङ्क्ते॥140॥

The one who knows the cow's nature gets the milk.

क्षुद्रे गुह्यप्रकाशनमात्मवान् न कुर्यात्॥141॥

A good one should not reveal a secret to a mean one.

आश्रितैरप्यवमत्यते मृदुस्वभावः॥142॥

The soft-natured one is disregarded even by those dependent on him.

तीक्ष्णदण्डः सर्वैरुद्वेजनीयो भवति॥143॥

The one who metes out severe punishment creates agitation in everyone.

यथार्हदण्डकारी स्यात्॥144॥

Apt punishment should be meted out.

अल्पसारं श्रुतवन्तमपि न बहु मन्यते लोकः॥145॥

A weak (ruler), even if learned, is not respected by people.

अतिभारः पुरुषमवसादयति॥146॥

Excessive burden overpowers a person.

यः संसदि परदोषं शंसति स स्वदोषं प्रख्यापयति॥147॥

He who speaks of others' faults in an assembly proclaims his own defect.

आत्मानमेव नाशयत्यनात्मवतां कोपः॥148॥

One who cannot control himself is destroyed by his anger.

प्रतयक्षपरोक्षानुमानैः कार्याणि परीक्षेत॥132॥

Things should be examined with reference to facts, patent and latent, and inferences.

अपरीक्ष्यकारिणं श्रीः परित्यजति॥133॥

Prosperity forsakes one who does things without proper examination.

परीक्ष्य तार्या विपत्तिः॥134॥

Danger should be overcome after proper analysis.

स्वशक्तिं ज्ञात्वा कार्यमारभेत॥135॥

One should begin a venture after assessing one's strength.

स्वजनं तर्पयित्वा यः शेषभोजी सोऽमृतभोजी॥136॥

He feeds on nectar who first feeds his people and then eats the left-overs.

सर्वानुष्ठज्ञनादायमुखानि वर्धन्ते॥137॥

By undertaking all kinds of activities, the ways to profit develop.

नास्ति भीरोः कार्यचिन्ता॥138॥

The coward does not think of action.

स्वामिनः शीलं ज्ञात्वा कार्यार्यी कार्य साधयेत्॥139॥

The favour-seeker accomplishes his end after knowing the nature of his master.

स्वभावो दुरतिक्रमः॥327॥

It is difficult to change intrinsic nature.

अपराधानुरूपो दण्डः॥328॥

Punishment should befit the crime.

कथानुरूपं प्रतिवचनम्॥329॥

Retort should befit the question.

विभवानुरूपमाभरणम्॥330॥

Adornment should befit resources.

कुलानुरूपं वृत्तम्॥331॥

Conduct should befit family.

कार्यानुरूपः प्रयत्नः॥332॥

Effort should befit the task.

पात्रानुरूपं दानम्॥333॥

Donation should befit recipient.

वयोऽनुरूपो वेषः॥334॥

Dress should befit age.

स्वाम्यनुकूलो भृत्यः॥335॥

Servant should obey the master.

दैवं शान्तिकर्मणा प्रतिषेद्धव्यम्॥123॥

Destiny has to be counteracted through propitiatory deeds.

मानुषीं कार्यविपत्तिं कौशलेन विनिवारयेत्॥124॥

Man-made obstacles should be overcome through one's skill.

कार्यविपत्तौ दोषान् वर्णयन्ति बालिशाः॥125॥

When things get into difficulties, the childish describe the handicaps.

कार्यार्थिना दाक्षिण्यं न कर्त्तव्यम्॥126॥

Those who seek to achieve things should show no mercy.

क्षीरार्थी वत्सो मातुरूधः प्रतिहन्ति॥127॥

The milk-seeking calf strikes at the mother's udders.

अप्रयत्नात् कार्यविपत्तिर्भवेत्॥128॥

Due to lack of effort tasks fail.

न दैवप्रमाणानां कार्यसिद्धिः॥129॥

Those who blindly believe in destiny do not achieve anything.

कार्यबाह्यो न पोषयत्याश्रितान्॥130॥

An inactive person cannot protect those who seek refuge in him.

यः कार्यं न पश्यति सोऽन्धः॥131॥

He who does not see action is blind.

दुर्बलोऽपि राजा नावमन्तव्यः॥87॥

A ruler, even if weak, should not be despised.

नास्त्यग्नेदौर्वल्यम्॥88॥

Fire has no weakness.

दण्डे प्रतीयते वृत्तिः॥89॥

All activity is understood in wielding the sceptre.

वृत्तिमूलमर्थलाभः।।90।।

Acquisition of wealth has its root in activity.

अर्थमूलौ धर्मकामौ।।91।।

Righteousness and pleasures have their root in wealth.

अर्थमूलं कार्यम्।।92।।

Work is the root of wealth.

यदल्पप्रयत्नात् कार्यसिद्धिर्भवति।।93।।

A little effort accomplishes the task.

उपायपूर्वं न दुष्करं स्यात्।।94।।

A task in which an expedient is used is not difficult to achieve.

अनुपायपूर्वं कार्यं कृतमपि नश्यति।।95।।

If no expedient is used, task, even if attempted, fails.

कार्यार्थिनामुपाय एव सहायः।।96।।

Expedient is the aid to those who seek success in undertaking.

कार्यं पुरुषकारेण लक्ष्यं सम्पद्यते।।97।।

A task attains its objective through human effort.

पुरुषकारमनुवर्तते दैवम्।।98।।

Fortune follows human effort.

दैवं विनाऽतिप्रयत्नं करोति यत् तद् विफलम्।।99।।

Without God's grace, even excessive effort proves fruitless.

असमाहितस्य वृत्तिर्न विद्यते॥100॥

One who is not calm and collected cannot accomplish tasks.

पूर्वं निश्चित्य पश्चात् कार्यमारभेत॥101॥

One should decide first and then commence the task.

कार्यान्तरे दीर्घसूत्रता न कर्त्तव्या॥102॥

There should be no delay in the undertaking of a new task after completing one.

न चलचित्तस्य कार्यावाप्तिः॥103॥

The fickle-minded one does not accomplish tasks.

हस्तगतावमाननात् कार्यव्यतिक्रमो भवति॥104॥

If what is obtained is despised, things go awry.

काम्यैर्विशेशैरूपचरणमुपचारः॥345॥

Provision of desirable services is courtesy.

चिरपरिचितानामत्युपचारः शंकितव्य॥346॥

Excessive courtesy from long-known persons is suspicious.

गौर्दुष्करा श्वसहस्रादेकाकिनी श्रेयसी॥347॥

Even an ordinary cow is superior to a thousand dogs.

श्वो मयूरादद्य कपोतो वरः॥348॥

A pigeon today is better than a peacock tomorrow.

अतिसंगो दोषमुत्पादयति॥349॥

Excessive companionship creates trouble.

सर्वं जयत्यक्रोधः॥350॥

The one without anger wins over all.

यद्यपकारिणि कोपः कोपे कोप एव कर्त्तव्यः॥351॥

If one feels angry with a harmful person, one should be angry with anger itself. (Anger towards harming persons should not be displayed openly.)

मतिमत्सु मूर्खमित्रगुरुवल्लभेषु विवादो न कर्त्तव्यः॥352॥

One should not argue with the intelligent, the foolish, friends, teachers and the beloved.

स्त्रियोऽपि स्त्रैणमवमन्यते॥318॥

Even women despise womanizers.

न पुष्पार्थी सिंचति शुष्कतरुम्॥319॥

One desirous of flowers does not water a dry tree.

अद्रव्यप्रयत्नो बालुकाक्वथनादनन्यः॥320॥

Attempting a task without resources is like ploughing the sand.

न महाजनहासः कर्त्तव्यः॥321॥

One should not laugh at great people.

कार्यससम्पदं निमित्तानि सूचयन्ति॥322॥

Omens indicate the success or failure of tasks undertaken.

नक्षत्रादपि निमित्तानि विशेषयन्ति॥323॥

Rational prognostics are superior to stars (in guidance).

न त्वरितस्य नक्षत्रपरीक्षा॥324॥

One who desires speedy accomplishment of tasks does not look to the stars (to know his fortune).

परिचये दोषा न छाद्यन्ते॥325॥

In familiarity, flaws do not remain hidden.

स्व्यमशुद्धः परानाशंकते।326॥

The impure ones suspect others.

यावच्छत्रोश्छिद्रं पश्यति तावद्धस्तेन वा स्कन्धेन वा बाह्यः॥193॥

Till the enemy's weakness is known, he should be kept on friendly terms.

शत्रुंछिद्रे प्रहरेत्॥194॥

An enemy should be struck at his weak point.

आत्मच्छिद्र न प्रकाशयेत्॥195॥

One's weakness should not be revealed.

छिद्रप्रहारिणः शत्रवः॥196॥

Enemies strike at weak spots.

हस्तगतमपि शत्रुं न विश्वसेत्॥197॥

Even a captured enemy should not be trusted.

स्वजनस्य दुर्वृत्तं निवारयेत्॥198॥

Wrongful activities of one's people should be stopped.

स्वजनावमानोऽपि मनस्विनां दुःखमावहति॥199॥

The disgrace of one's people brings sorrow to the noble-minded.

एकाङ्गदोषः पुरुषमवसादयति॥200॥

The defect in one limb ruins a man.

शत्रुं जयति सुवृत्तता॥201॥

Good behaviour wins even an enemy.

इन्द्रियाणां प्रशमं शास्त्रम्॥300॥

Learning makes the senses peaceful.

अशास्त्रकार्यवृत्तौ शास्त्रांकुशं निवारयति॥301॥

The goad of learning corrects those engaged in unworthy deeds.

नीचस्य विद्या नोपेतव्या॥302॥

One should not learn the learning of the low-minded.

म्लेच्छभाषणं न शिक्षेत॥303॥

Low language should not be learnt.

म्लेच्च्छानामपि सुवृत्तं ग्राह्यम्॥304॥

Good customs of even low people should be adopted.

गुणो न मत्सरः कर्त्तव्यः॥305॥

One should not envy others' good qualities.

शत्रोरपि सुगुणो ग्राह्यः॥306॥

A good quality should be learnt even from an enemy.

विषादप्यमृत्तं ग्राह्यम्॥307॥

Nectar should be extracted even from poison.

अवस्थया पुरुषः सम्मान्यते॥308॥

A person is honoured according to his status.

निरुत्साहाद् दैवं पतति॥185॥

Due to lack of effort, fortune fails.

मत्स्यार्थीव जलमुपयुज्यार्थं गृह्लीयात्॥186॥

Utilizable resources should be captured, as the fisherman catches fish from water.

अविश्वस्तेषु विश्वासो न कर्त्तव्यः॥187॥

The untrustworthy should not be trusted.

विषं विषमेव सर्वकालम्॥188॥

Poison is always poison.

अर्थसमादाने वैरिणां सङ्ग एव न कर्त्तव्यः॥189॥

In the acquisition of wealth, the association of enemies should be avoided.

अर्थसिद्धौ वैरिणं न विश्वसेत्॥190॥

Even after wealth has been acquired, an enemy should not be trusted.

अर्थाधीन एव नियतसम्बन्धः॥191॥

A permanent relationship is dependent on wealth.

शत्रोरपि सुतः सखा रक्षितव्यः॥192॥

A friend, even if he be the enemy's son, should be protected.

गुणवदाश्रयान्निर्गुणोऽपि गुणी भवति॥176॥

Through the association of the good, even one without virtue becomes virtuous.

क्षीराश्रित जलं क्षीरमेव भवति॥177॥

Water mixed with milk becomes milk.

मृत्पिण्डोऽपि पाटलिगन्धमुत्पादयति॥178॥

Even a lump of earth can produce the smell of the trumpet flower.

रजतं कनकसङ्गात् कनकं भवति॥179॥

Silver in contact with gold becomes golden.

उपकर्तर्यपकर्तुमिच्छत्यबुधः॥180॥

The foolish wish to do harm to those who do good.

न पापकर्मणामाक्रोशभायम्॥181॥

Evil doers are not afraid of criticism.

उत्साहवतां शत्रवोऽपि वशीभवन्ति॥182॥

The enthusiastic ones win over even enemies.

विक्रमधना राजानः॥183॥

Valour is the wealth of rulers.

नास्त्यलसस्यैहिकामुष्मिकम्॥184॥

A lazy one cannot attain happiness in this world or the other.

बालादप्यर्थजातं श्रृणुयात्॥167॥

Meaningful words, even from a child, should be listened to.

सत्यमप्यश्रद्धेयं न वदेत्॥168॥

That which will not be believed, even if it is truth, should not be spoken.

नाल्पदोषाद् बहुगुणास्त्यजयन्ते॥169॥

Many qualities are not to be overlooked for a minor defect.

विपश्चित्स्वपि सुलभा दोषाः॥170॥

Faults are common even among the learned.

नास्ति रत्नमखण्डितम्॥171॥

There is no unbroken diamond.

मर्यादातीतं न कदाचिदपि विश्वसेत्॥172॥

Excessive courtesy should never be trusted.

अप्रिये कृतं प्रियमपि द्वेष्यं भवति॥173॥

In the case of an enemy, even a good gesture becomes harmful.

नमन्त्यपि तुलाकोटिः कूपोदकक्षयं करोति॥174॥

Even while bending, the mouth of the pitcher depletes the water in the well.

सतां मतं नातिक्रमेत्॥175॥

One should not act against the advice of the good.

तद्विपरीतोऽनर्थसेवी॥158॥

Acting against virtue and wealth is courting disaster.

ऋजुस्वभावपरो जनेषु दुर्लभः॥153॥

Honest and upright people are rare.

अवमानेनागतमैश्वर्यमवमन्यते साधुः॥160॥

The virtuous one despises prosperity attained through ignominy.

बहूनपि गुणानेको दोषो ग्रसति॥161॥

A single defect overshadows many qualities.

महात्मना परेण साहस न कर्त्तव्यम्॥162॥

Rash aggression should not be committed against a great and noble enemy.

कदाचिदपि चरित्रं न लंघयेत्॥163॥

The bounds of good conduct should never be crossed.

क्षुधार्तो न तृणं चरति सिंहः॥164॥

The lion, even if hungry, does not graze grass.

प्राणादपि प्रत्ययो रक्षितव्यः॥165॥

Trust should be kept even by sacrificing one's life.

पिशुनः श्रोता पुत्रदारैरपि त्यज्यते॥166॥

A slanderous listener is forsaken even by his wife and children.

नास्त्यप्राप्यं सत्यवताम्॥149॥

Nothing is unattainable by the truthful.

साहसेन न कार्यसिद्धिर्भवति॥150॥

Rashness does not accomplish tasks.

व्यसनार्तो विस्मरत्यप्रवेशेन॥151॥

The one troubled by calamities forgets them the moment they disappear.

नास्त्यनन्तरायः कालविक्षेपे॥152॥

When opportunities are lost, obstacles definitely arise.

असंशयविनाशात् संशयविनाशः श्रेयान्॥153॥

Doubtful ruin is better than definite ruin.

परधनानि निक्षेप्तुः केवलं स्वार्थम्॥154॥

Custody of others' riches is undertaken purely out of selfishness.

दानं धर्मः॥155॥

Donation is righteousness.

नार्यागतोऽर्थवद् विपरीतोऽनर्थभावः॥156॥

The opposite (that is non-donation) forebodes disaster, like wealth of the ignoble.

यो धर्मार्थौ न विवर्धयति स कामः॥157॥

That which does not increase virtue and wealth is lust.

नार्थिष्ववज्ञा कार्या॥437॥

Aid-seekers should not be hated.

दुष्कर कर्म कारयित्वा कर्तारमवमन्यते नीचः॥438॥

The evil one after propelling evil action, derides the doer.

नाकृतज्ञस्य नरकान्निवर्तनम्॥439॥

The ungrateful cannot escape hell.

जिह्वायत्तौ वृद्धिविनाशौ॥440॥

Development and decline depend on the tongue.

विषामृतयोराकरी जिह्वा॥441॥

Thc tongue is the storehouse of poison and nectar.

प्रियवादिनो न शत्रुः॥442॥

The sweet-spoken have no enemies.

स्तुता अपि देवतास्तुष्यन्ति॥443॥

Even gods, when praised, are pleased.

अनृतमपि दुर्वचनं चिरं तिष्ठति।।444।।

Evil speech, though unintended, remains long in memory.

राजद्विष्टं न च वक्तव्यम्।।445।।

Nothing antagonizing the ruler should be spoken.

सत्याद् देवो वर्षति।।420।।

Because of truth, God gives rain.

नानृतात् पालकं परम्।।421।।

There is no greater sin than untruth.

न मीमांस्या गुरवः।।422।।

Teachers should not be criticized.

खलत्वं नोपेयात्।।423।।

Villainy should not be tolerated.

नास्ति खलस्य मित्रम्।।424।।

The wicked have no friends.

लोकयात्रा दरिद्रं बाधते।।425।।

The poor find it hard to live.

अतिशूरो दानशूरः।।426।।

The most valiant is the valiant giver.

गुरुदेवब्राह्मणेषु भक्तिर्भूषणम्।।427।।

Devotion to teacher, God and the learned is adornment (for all).

सर्वस्य भूषणं विनयः।।428।।

Humility is everyone's adornment.

अकुलीनोऽपि विनीतः कुलीनाद् विशिष्टः॥429॥

Even a low-born one, if humble, is superior to an (arrogant) high-born one.

आचारादायुर्वर्धते कीर्तिश्च॥430॥

Good living enhances life-span and reputation.

प्रियमप्यहितं न वक्तव्यम्॥431॥

Sweet words, if inapt, should not be spoken.

बहुजनविरुद्धमेकं नानुवर्तेत॥432॥

One who is opposed by many people should not be followed.

न दुर्जनेषु भागधेयः कर्त्तव्यः॥433॥

One's fortune should not be linked to evil ones.

न कृतार्थेषु नीचेषु सम्बन्धः॥434॥

One should not associate with the low-minded, even if they are successful.

ऋणशत्रुव्याधिष्वशेषः कर्त्तव्यः॥435॥

Nothing should be allowed to remain in the case of: debts, enemies and disease. (There should be total extermination.)

भूत्यानुवर्तनं पुरुषस्य रसायनम्॥436॥

Treading the right path is man's best medicine.

नास्ति हव्यस्य व्याघातः॥515॥

A sacrificial offering to the gods is never lost.

शत्रुर्मित्रवत् प्रतिभाति॥516॥

An enemy can look like a friend.

मृगतृष्णा जलवद् भाति॥517॥

The mirage looks like water.

दुर्मेधसामसच्छास्त्रं मोहयति॥518॥

Evil sciences fascinate evil-minded ones.

सत्संगः स्वर्गवासः॥519॥

Company of the good is like residence in heaven.

आर्यः स्वमिव परं मन्यते॥520॥

The noble one deems others to be himself.

रूपानुवर्ती गुणः॥521॥

Quality conforms to appearance.

यत्र सुखेन वर्तते तदेव स्थानम्॥522॥

That is the ideal place where one can remain happily.

विश्वासघातिनो न निष्कृतिः॥523॥

Those who betray trust have no salvation.

दैन्यान्मरणमुत्तमम्॥506॥

Death is preferable to poverty.

आशा लज्जां व्यपोहति॥507॥

Desire dispels shame.

न मात्रा सह वासः कर्त्तव्यः॥508॥

One should not stay alone even with one's mother.

न दिवा स्वप्नं कुर्यात्॥510॥

One should not daydream.

न चासन्नमपि पश्यत्यैश्वर्यान्धो न शृणोतीष्टं वाक्यम्॥511॥

The one blinded by prosperity does not see the imminent nor listens to sane advice.

तदनुवर्तनमुभय सुखम्॥513॥

Acting according to the husband's wishes bestows material and spiritual happiness.

अतिथिमभ्यागतं पूजयेद् यथाविधि॥514॥

The guest who has come should be treated properly.

निम्बफलं काकैरेव भुज्यते॥497॥

The bitter neem fruit is eaten only by crows.

नाम्भोधिस्तृष्णामपोहति॥498॥

The ocean cannot quench thirst.

बालुका अपि स्वगुणमाश्रयन्ते॥499॥

Even sand conforms to its quality.

सन्तोऽसत्सु न रमन्ते॥500॥

Good people do not enjoy (the company of) evil ones.

हंसः प्रेतवने न रमते॥501॥

Swans do not like (to stay in) cremation grounds.

अर्थार्थं प्रवर्तते लोकः॥502॥

The world functions for the sake of money.

आशया बध्यते लोकः॥503॥

All worldly beings are bound by desire.

न चाशापरैः श्रीः सह तिष्ठति॥504॥

Prosperity does not stay with one ever immersed in desire.

आशापरे न धैर्यम्॥505॥

Those who have excessive desire have no firmness.

तपस्विनः पूजनीयाः॥411॥

Saints should be worshipped.

परदारान्न गच्छेत्॥412॥

Others' wives should not be sought.

अन्नदानं भ्रूणहत्यामपि मार्ष्टि॥413॥

Gift of food wipes out even the sin of infanticide.

न वेदबाह्यो धर्मः॥414॥

There is no righteous duty, not specified in the learned scriptures.

कदाचिदपि र्धं निषेवेत्॥415॥

Righteousness should be practised always.

स्वर्गं नयति सूनृतम्॥416॥

Truth leads one to heaven.

नास्ति सत्यात् परं तपः॥417॥

There is no penance greater than (the observance of) truth.

सत्यं स्वर्गस्य साधनम्॥418॥

Truth is the means to heaven.

सत्येन धार्यते लोकः॥419॥

The world is borne by truth.

गुरुवशानुवर्ती शिष्यः॥337॥

A student should obey the teacher.

पितृवशानुवर्ती पुत्रः॥338॥

A son should obey the father.

अत्युपचारः शंकितव्यः॥339॥

Excessive courtesy should be suspected.

(स्वामिनि कुपिते) स्वामिनमेवानुवर्तेत॥340॥

When the master is angry, he should be obeyed.

मातृताडितो वत्सो मातारमेवानुरोदिति॥341॥

A child beaten by the mother cries only before the mother.

स्नेहवतः स्वल्पो हि रोषः॥342॥

The anger of the affectionate is short-lived.

आत्मच्छिद्रं न पश्यति परच्छिद्रमेव पश्यति बालिशः॥343॥

The fool sees others' faults, not his own.

सोपचारः कैतवः॥344॥

Cunning accompanies courtesy.

नास्त्यपिशाचमैश्वर्यम्॥353॥

There is no undevilish prosperity.

नास्ति धनवतां शुभकर्मसु श्रमः॥354॥

It is not difficult for the rich to do good deeds.

नास्ति गतिश्रमो यानवताम्॥355॥

The ones who travel by carriage do not feel the weariness of journeys.

यो यस्मिन् कुशलः स तस्मिन् योक्तव्यः॥357॥

Each one should be entrusted with the job in which he is skilled.

न कदाऽपि देवताऽवमन्तव्या॥402॥

Deities should never be despised.

न चक्षुषः समं ज्योतिरस्ति॥403॥

There is no light equal to eyesight.

चक्षुर्हि शरीरिणां नेता॥404॥

The eye is the leader of the embodied being.

अपचक्षुषः किं शरीरेण॥405॥

What is the use of the body for the blind?

यथा शरीरं तथा ज्ञानम्॥408॥

A sound intellect in a sound body.

यथा बुद्धिस्तथा विभवः॥409॥

Prosperity depends on the intellect.

अग्नावग्निं न निक्षिपेत्॥410॥

One should not deposit fire in fire. (One should not express anger at the mighty.)

Bibliography

Kautilyarthasastra of Sri Vishnugupta, Pub. Oriental Research Institute, University of Mysore, 1960.

The Kautilya Arthasastra (Parts I, II and III), R.P. Kangle, Pub. University of Bombay, 1963.

Chanakya Rajaniti, Edited by Ludwik Sternback, Pub. The Adyar Library and Research Centre, 1963.

Age of the Nandas and Mauryas, Edited by K.A. Nilakanta Sastri, Pub. Motilal Banarsidass, Banaras.

A Comprehensive History of India, Vol. II, *The Mauryas and Satavahanas 325 B.C.-A.D. 300,* Edited by K.A. Nilakanta Sastri, Pub. Orient Longmans.

Kautilyarthasastrasangraha and the Nitisutras of Brihaspati, Chanakya, and Somadeva, Edited by Vidwan N.S. Venkatanathacharya, Pub. University of Mysore.

Mudra Rakshasa by Visakhadatta, Edited by K.T. Telang, Pub. Bombay Sanskrit Series, Tukaram Javaji, Bombay, 1915.

Some Aspects of Kautilya's Political Thinking by Dr. Radhagobinda Basak.

The *Mudraraksasanatakakatha of Mahadeva,* Edited by Dr. V. Raghavan, Pub. The Sarasvati Mahal Series, T.M.S.S.M. Library, Tanjore, 1971.

Arthasastra of Jayamangala, Edited by G. Harihara Sastri, Kuppuswami Sastri Research Institute, Mylapore, Madras, 1958.

Kalidasa and Kautilya, Article by Dr. V. Raghavan, 1946, Prepared for All India Oriental Conference Thirteenth Session, Nagpur University.

Kautilya's Arthasastra, Translated by Dr. R. Shamasastry, Fifth Edition, 1956.

Chanakya and the Arthasastra by Somnath Dhar, Pub. The Indian Institute of World Culture, Bangalore.

Chanakya Rajanitisastram by Sunitikumar Pathak, Pub. Visva-Bharati, Santiniketan.